CONTEMPORARY SEASIDE HOUSES
MAISONS MODERNES DE BORD DE MER
TRAUMHÄUSER AM MEER

CONTEMPORARY SEASIDE HOUSES
MAISONS MODERNES DE BORD DE MER
TRAUMHÄUSER AM MEER

EVERGREEN

EVERGREEN is an imprint of

Taschen GmbH

© 2006 TASCHEN GmbH

Hohenzollernring 53, D-50672 Köln

www.taschen.com

Editor Editrice Redakteur:
Simone Schleifer

English translation Traduction anglaise Englische Übersetzung:
Matthew Clarke

French translation Traduction française Französische Übersetzung:
Marion Westerhoff

German translation Traduction allemande Deutsche Übersetzung:
Susanne Engler

Proof reading Relecture Korrektur:
Marie-Pierre Santamarina, Martin Rolshoven

Art director Direction artistique Art Direktor:
Mireia Casanovas Soley

Graphic design and layout Mise en page et maquette Graphische Gestaltung und Layout:
Elisabet Rodríguez

Printed by Imprimé par Gedruckt durch:
Gráficas Toledo, Spain

ISBN-13: 978-3-8228-2787-1
ISBN-10: 3-8228-2787-8

Contents   Index   Inhalt

Building a beach house is one of the most appealing projects both for the architects and the future inhabitants, as it responds to the basic necessity of humanity to be consistent with nature. As human beings, we have become conscious of our need to refer to this necessity in order to make sense of our existence in an increasingly complex world. Architecture intends to do just that.

The beach landscape has special characteristics. As the boundary between the land and the sea, the terrain is subject to extreme weather conditions. Within the space of just a few hours, the intensity of the sun or wind can change drastically. At the same time, the large mass of water functions as a thermostat to absorb the heat during the day and to give it off at night, producing minimal fluctuations in temperature. The vegetation is also punished by the extreme climate and features formal characteristics. The flora might include tall, svelte palm trees or large, tree-like masses ranging from dense forests to small shrubs that are placed like a cover above the topography. Finally, the rocky geography creates complicated situations and the presence of sand causes continuous changes in the level of the ground. These fascinating and natural, though difficult to tackle conditions of the coast are the framework for the projects included in this book.

The respect for seaside topography has led to such architectural solutions as raising a house on pillars, widening openings to the utmost in areas lacking in sunlight, or closing off the house to protect it from strong winds. The volumetric dimensions and relationships between the structures that form the projects are generally short in height when the proportions of the site permit it. What dominates is a fragmented composition that creates a multitude of volumes and exterior spaces, achieving a better relationship with the exterior but also helping to make the project's different areas independent.

This book is a collection of projects of renowned architects from all over the world, each one revealing a unique dialogue between architecture and the ocean.

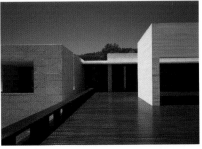

Construire une maison au bord de la mer est un pari très intéressant tant pour l'architecte que pour le client, car c'est une perspective qui répond au besoin fondamental de l'humanité d'être conforme à la nature. L'homme a parfaitement pris conscience de l'urgence de reconnaître cette nécessité pour que son existence trouve un sens dans un monde toujours plus complexe, et c'est bien ce à quoi tend l'architecture.

Le paysage côtier est un milieu aux caractéristiques déterminantes. Frontière entre la terre et la mer, le terrain s'expose à des conditions climatiques extrêmes. En l'espace de quelques heures, l'intensité du soleil ou du vent peut changer du tout au tout. De son côté, l'énorme masse d'eau agit comme un thermostat qui absorbe la chaleur pendant la journée pour la relâcher ensuite pendant la nuit, en produisant des fluctuations de température minimes. La végétation subit également les attaques d'un climat extrême, et présente des caractéristiques qui lui sont propres : la flore qui revêt les côtes est constituée de palmiers élancés et sveltes dans les zones tropicales ou de grandes étendues arborées allant des bois denses aux petits arbustes des climats de l'Arctique. Ajoutons enfin, qu'un terrain à typologie rocheuse engendre des enclaves escarpées, difficiles à appréhender et que la présence de sable provoque des fluctuations constantes au niveau du sol. Ces conditions naturelles, défis d'architecture exaltants, forment la trame des projets présentés dans ce livre.

Le souci de respecter l'environnement naturel d'un milieu aussi spectaculaire que celui-ci, a conduit les professionnels à rechercher des solutions architecturales extrêmes : élever la construction sur pilotis, élargir les ouvertures au maximum dans les zones à faible ensoleillement ou fermer une maison et l'envelopper sur elle-même pour la protéger de la violence des vents. Les dimensions volumétriques et la distribution des programmes domestiques dépendent également de tous ces paramètres. Néanmoins, il en résulte essentiellement une composition fragmentée qui génère une multitude de volumes et d'espaces externes, en quête d'une relation idéale avec l'environnement extérieur, sans nuire à l'indépendance des différentes zones qui composent le projet.

Pour offrir au lecteur un large éventail de cette architecture exceptionnelle, cet ouvrage réunit une sélection de projets d'architectes renommés du monde entier, où chacun d'entre eux fait apparaître un dialogue unique entre l'architecture et la mer.

 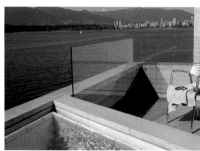  

Die Errichtung eines Hauses am Meer ist sowohl für den Architekten als auch für den Kunden eine interessante Herausforderung, da man bei der Planung auf die grundlegende Notwendigkeit der Menschheit eingehen muss, konsequent mit der Natur umzugehen. Der Mensch ist sich mittlerweile absolut darüber im Klaren, dass es unerlässlich ist, die Natur zu schützen und zu bewahren, damit seine Existenz in dieser immer komplexeren Welt noch einen Sinn hat.

Die Küstenlandschaft ist eine Umgebung, die sehr besondere Charakterzüge aufweist. Sie bildet die Grenze zwischen dem Land und dem Meer und ist oft sehr extremen Witterungsverhältnissen ausgesetzt. In nur wenigen Stunden kann sich die Stärke der Sonne oder des Windes drastisch ändern. Gleichzeitig wirkt sich die enorme Wassermasse ausgleichend auf die Temperatur aus; sie nimmt tagsüber Wärme auf und gibt sie nachts ab, so dass die Temperaturunterschiede geringer als im Inland sind. Die Vegetation ist sehr extremen Wetterverhältnissen ausgesetzt, so dass sich eine eigene Pflanzenwelt an der Küste entwickelt hat. An tropischen Küsten findet man hohe und schlanke Tannen, in kälteren Regionen große Wälder und in den arktischen Gebieten kleine Sträucher. Meist ist das Gelände felsig, so dass abrupte Höhenunterschiede entstehen, die das Bauen stark erschweren. An sandigen Küsten kann sich die Bodenhöhe ständig verändern. Diese Umweltbedingungen stellen eine faszinierende Herausforderung an die Architekten dar, und sie bilden den Rahmen für die Häuser, die in diesem Buch vorgestellt werden.

Der Wunsch, diese natürliche und so beeindruckende Umgebung so weit wie möglich zu respektieren, hat zu extremen architektonischen Lösungen geführt wie z. B. die Errichtung eines Hauses auf Säulen, in Zonen, in denen es wenig Sonnenlicht gibt, die Fenster so groß wie möglich zu machen oder ein Haus zu schließen und zu umhüllen, um es vor den starken Winden zu schützen. Die Größe der Gebäudeteile und die Anordnung der Zimmer hängt ebenfalls von diesen Parametern ab. Zurzeit dominiert sicherlich ein Baustil, der aus einer Reihe von Gebäudeteilen und Außenbereichen besteht, durch die eine intensive Beziehung zur Umgebung geschaffen wird, ohne dabei die Unabhängigkeit der verschiedenen Bereiche zu beeinträchtigen.

Um unseren Lesern diese einzigartige Architektur in ihrer Vielfältigkeit vorzustellen, enthält dieser Band eine Auswahl an Häusern berühmter Architekten der ganzen Welt, die eins gemeinsam haben: den einzigartigen Dialog zwischen der Architektur und dem Meer.

Portas Novas House

Maison Portas Novas

Haus Portas Novas

The architect managed to adapt this house perfectly to the lay of the land by drawing it up with three vertices that coincide with the boundary of the lot and endowing it with splendid views of the tropical setting that surrounds it. The east façade gives on to a slope covered with trees, while the Pacific Ocean can be glimpsed from the opposite side. To the south, the house opens up on to the sea in a series of steps, while to the north it enjoys an uninterrupted view of the sea, complete with small islets in the foreground. The main volume comprises three modules separated by two beds of silica and wooden walkways. The central module, which contains the sitting room, serves as a vantage point, on account of its raised position and glass façade.

L'architecte a réussi une intégration parfaite à la topographie du terrain en concevant cette habitation dont les trois sommets coïncident avec les marges de délimitation du terrain, instaurant une perspective privilégiée sur l'environnement tropical qui l'entoure. La façade est affiche une pente arborée, le côté opposé s'ouvrant sur le Pacifique. Du coté sud, la maison s'ouvre en s'échelonnant vers la mer qui, au nord, s'offre à l'infini, avec des petits îlots au premier plan. Le corps principal comporte trois modules séparés par des parterres de silice et des passerelles de bois. Le module central, avec la salle de séjour, sert de bastion panoramique de par sa situation en hauteur et sa façade vitrée.

Der Architekt passte dieses Haus perfekt an die Bodenform des Geländes an. Dies erreichte er durch drei Scheitelpunkte, die mit der Trennlinie der Ränder des Grundstücks übereinstimmen und einen wundervollen Blick über die tropische Landschaft bieten, die das Gebäude umgibt. Die Ostfassade zeigt zu einem mit Bäumen bestandenen Abhang, während man von der anderen Seite aus auf den Pazifik schaut. Auf der Südseite öffnet sich das Haus stufenförmig in Richtung Meer, und im Norden hat man einen weiten Blick über den Ozean. Im Vordergrund sieht man einige kleine Felseninseln. Der Hauptkörper des Gebäudes besteht aus drei Modulen, die durch Gartenbeete mit Kieseln und Laufstege aus Holz getrennt sind. Das zentrale Modul, in dem sich das Wohnzimmer befindet, bildet eine Art Bollwerk mit Panoramablick, da es erhöht liegt und eine verglaste Fassade besitzt.

All the daytime areas serve as vantage points, on account of the expanse of glass sheltering them from the exterior.

Toutes les zones de jour sont en elles-mêmes à l'image d'un mirador de par l'importance des surfaces vitrées qui les protègent de l'extérieur.

Alle über den Tag genutzten Wohnbereiche stellen an sich schon eine Art Aussichtsterrasse dar, da es viele verglaste Flächen gibt, die vor Wettereinflüssen schützen.

Water is present in the very architecture of the building, setting up a delightful interplay of visual and acoustic effects.

L'eau est présente au coeur même de l'architecture de l'édifice, créant un charmant jeu de sensations visuelles et auditives.

Das Element Wasser bildet selbst einen Teil der Architektur. Die Bewohner können sich am Anblick und am Klang dieses Elementes erfreuen.

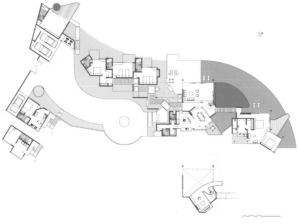

› Location plan Plan de situation Umgebungsplan

Shaw House
Maison Shaw
Shaw Haus

This 3,070-sq.-ft house on English Bay benefits from superb panoramic views of the mountains overlooking Vancouver. The narrowness of the lot—measuring 32 ft by 158 ft—meant that the living area was only 27 feet wide once construction requirements had been taken into account; this obliged the architects to come up with an unconventional design that exploited space vertically and stretched out toward the sea. The house is spread over three levels: a basement and two stories. The limited dimensions of the lot made it difficult to install the swimming pool at ground level without depriving the lower level of space, so it was situated on the top level, along the west side of the house, as if it had been superimposed onto the landscape. This pool has a terrace at each end—reached via the bedroom and the study, respectively—offering an array of magnificent views.

Cette résidence de 285 m² située à English Bay bénéficie de splendides vues sur les montagnes qui dominent l'horizon de Vancouver. Le terrain étroit, 10 m de large par 48 m de profondeur, a été réduit à 8 mètres de large, suite aux contraintes spatiales. L'étroitesse du terrain a poussé les architectes à exploiter l'espace à la verticale et vers la mer. Distribuée sur trois niveaux, la maison dispose d'un sous-sol et de deux étages. Due à l'étroite configuration du terrain, l'implantation de la piscine au niveau du sol était impossible, sous peine de réduire l'espace du rez-de-chaussée. Elle a donc été installée au niveau supérieur, le long du côté ouest de la maison, reliée aux deux bouts par deux terrasses communiquant avec la chambre à coucher et le studio. Cette piscine flottante semble se superposer au paysage, offrant des vues magnifiques que l'habitant peut admirer sous des angles multiples.

Von diesem 285 m² großen Haus in English Bay hat man einen wundervollen Blick auf die Berge am Horizont von Vancouver. Das schmale Grundstück ist nur 10 m breit, aber 48 m tief, so dass der Wohnbereich nicht breiter als 8 m sein durfte. Diese Grundstücksform zwang die Architekten zu einer sehr ungewöhnlichen Gestaltung. Der Platz musste vertikal und in Richtung Wasser ausgenutzt werden. Das dreistöckige Haus besitzt ein Untergeschoss und zwei Etagen. Aufgrund dieser Grundstücksform war es auch schwierig, einen Swimmingpool auf Bodenhöhe anzulegen, ohne dabei an Raum für das Untergeschoss einzubüßen. Deshalb wurde der Swimmingpool auf einer höheren Etage auf der Westseite des Hauses konstruiert, so dass seine beiden Enden mit Terrassen verbunden sind, die wiederum zu dem Schlaf- und Arbeitszimmer führen. Der schwebende Swimmingpool erhebt sich über die Landschaft, so dass man von verschiedenen Punkten aus eine herrliche Sicht hat.

The high risk of earthquakes in this area prompted an exhaustive study that determined the building's structure.

Vu le risque sismique élevé de cette zone, une étude exhaustive a du être réalisée pour déterminer la future structure de la construction.

Da in dieser Region ein hohes Erdbebenrisiko herrscht, wurden zunächst gründliche Studien durchgeführt, bevor man sich für eine Struktur entschied.

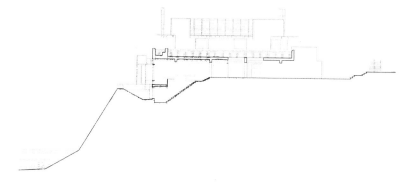

› Longitudinal section Section longitudinale Längsschnitt

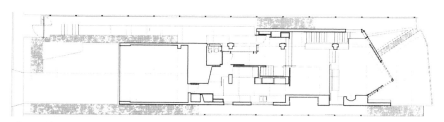

› Ground floor   Rez-de-chaussée   Erdgeschoss

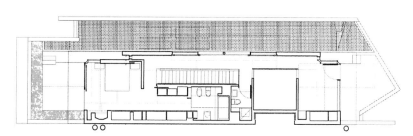

› First floor   Premier étage   Erstes Obergeschoss

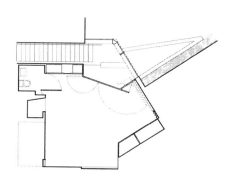

› Second floor   Deuxième étage   Zweites Obergeschoss

Gontovnik House
Maison Gontovnik
Haus Gontovnik

In this design, volume–so simple in its appearance–was the deciding factor when it came to solving the complex problems that arose from the location and topography. Although the site is an excellent one, it does not, for the most part, offer a good view of the sea. The land slopes up from the street side to the top of a rocky crag. The volume, therefore, has been sliced into different levels, giving the impression of a stairway rising up to a vantage point where there is a spectacular view of the Caribbean. The first "slice" or step of the building is down at street-level and contains the garages and private rooms. The next section up, the middle slice, is the entrance to the house and the place where the main corridors converge. It also contains the kitchen and the dining room, all arranged around a central patio. Finally, up on the crag, is the top slice, containing the living and master bedroom, both with windows that look out over the cliff.

La conception de cette habitation, d'une simplicité apparente, a su résoudre les problèmes complexes résultant de la situation et de la topographie de l'endroit, car malgré un emplacement idéal, il n'y avait pas de bonnes vues sur la mer. Le terrain s'élevant de la rue vers le haut d'un rocher, permit de concevoir différents niveaux à l'instar d'un escalier montant vers une position stratégique. Le premier étage de l'édifice, situé au niveau de la rue, abrite le garage et les pièces privées. La deuxième section ascendante, ou niveau intermédiaire, comprend l'entrée de l'habitation, le lieu où convergent les zones de circulation. La cuisine et la salle à manger sont disposées autour d'un patio central. En dernier, le salon et la chambre à coucher des propriétaires se partagent le niveau supérieur, bénéficiant ainsi d'une vue panoramique incomparable sur la falaise.

Die scheinbar sehr einfache Gestaltung dieses Hauses musste sich den komplexen Problemen stellen, die durch die Oberflächenform des Standortes entstanden, denn, obwohl das Grundstück sich in einer schönen Lage befindet, gab es keinen guten Blick auf das Meer. Das Grundstück steigt von der Straße bis nach oben auf einen Felsblock an. Deshalb wurden verschiedene Ebenen angelegt, die den Eindruck einer Treppe erwecken, die bis zu einem Aussichtspunkt ansteigt. Die erste Etage des Gebäudes liegt auf der Höhe der Straße. Hier befinden sich die Garage und die privaten Räume. In der darüber gelegenen Etage, dem Zwischengeschoss, befindet sich der Eingang zum Haus und der Ort, an dem die verschiedenen Durchgangsbereiche aufeinander treffen. Die Küche und das Speisezimmer umgeben den Innenhof. Im obersten Stockwerk befinden sich schließlich das Wohnzimmer und das große Schlafzimmer, von denen aus man den schönsten Blick auf die Klippen hat.

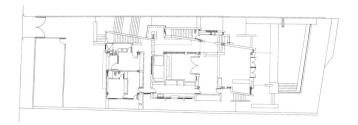

› Ground floor Rez-de-chaussée Erdgeschoss

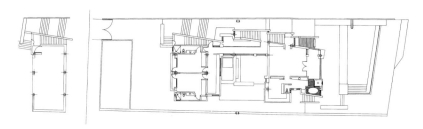

› First floor Premier étage Erstes Obergeschoss

Wood was the element chosen to break up the continuity established by the muted nature of both the colors and the other materials.

Le bois est le matériau sélectionné pour rompre la continuité de la palette sobre des matériaux comme des couleurs.

Die zurückhaltenden Farben und schlichten Materialien, die verwendet wurden, werden durch das Element Holz unterbrochen.

Residence on St. Andrews Beach

Résidence à St. Andrews Beach

Residenz in St. Andrews Beach

The dunes on the Mornington Peninsula form one of the most striking landscapes in Australia. In recent years, the erosion caused by the strong winds that lash the area has necessitated a program to plant tea trees to protect the dunes. This natural barrier inspired the architect when he drew up this single-story volume, which stands on pillars, facing the beach. On the north façade, a ramp leads to a walkway that provides access to the home. The south façade, fronted by all the daytime areas, is completely covered with glass, to enable the occupants to take advantage of the extensive vistas of the sea. The foot of this façade gives way to a wooden staircase that leads right down to the dunes.

Les plages de dunes de la péninsule de Mornington forment un des paysages les plus particuliers du continent australien. Dû à l'érosion produite par les vents violents qui frappent la zone, un programme de plantation de théiers a été entrepris au cours de ces dernières années afin de protéger les dunes. Cette barrière naturelle a inspiré l'architecte lors de la conception de ce volume d'un seul étage, ancré sur la plage et construit sur pilotis. Sur la façade nord, une rampe mène à une passerelle pour accéder à l'habitation. La façade sud, où se trouvent toutes les pièces de jour, est entièrement vitrée, permettant ainsi de jouir des grandes vues sur la mer. Au pied de cette façade, une échelle de bois mène aux dunes.

Die Strände voller Dünen auf der Halbinsel Mornington formen eine der eigentümlichsten Landschaften auf dem australischen Kontinent. Aufgrund der Erosion, die durch die starken Winde in der Region verursacht wird, wurde in den letzten Jahren ein Programm zum Pflanzen von Teebäumen durchgeführt, die die Dünen schützen sollen. Diese natürliche Barriere inspirierte den Architekten zu einem Haus mit einem einzigen Stockwerk, von dem aus man auf den Strand blickt und das von Säulen gestützt wird. An der Nordfassade führt eine Rampe auf einen Laufsteg, über den man das Haus erreicht. Die Südfassade, zu der alle tagsüber bewohnten Räume liegen, ist vollständig verglast, so dass man einen wundervollen Blick auf das Meer hat. Zu Füßen dieser Fassade liegt eine Freitreppe aus Holz, die in die Dünen führt.

The façade is fronted by glass along all its length to provide far-reaching views of the sea.

La façade sud est toute en verre et permet de bénéficier de splendides vues sur la mer.

Die Südfassade ist vollständig verglast und bietet so einen herrlichen Ausblick auf den Ozean.

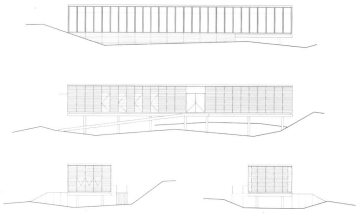

› Elevations Élévations Aufrisse

House in Cadaqués

Maison à Cadaqués

Haus in Cadaqués

The distinctive triangular shape and natural setting of this lot, perched on a cliff on the spectacular Costa Brava, influenced the approach to this project from the outset. The unbeatable location overlooking the sea and the enticing views—both close by and in the distance—encouraged the design of an open house, but the harsh winds that lash the area also called for protection. The shape of the lot gave rise to a triangular floor plan that takes in the living quarters and is completed by the garden and swimming pool, facing south to shield them from the wind and benefit from the splendid views of the sea and the bay of Cadaqués. The low elevation from the land and the use of materials like glass, anodized aluminum and stone from Cadaqués itself ensure that the house fits in harmoniously with the coastal landscape.

Juchée sur une falaise de la spectaculaire Costa Brava, l'environnement naturel de cette parcelle de terrain et sa forme triangulaire particulière définissent, d'emblée, la conception du projet. L'emplacement idyllique face à la mer et les vues proches et lointaines invitaient à concevoir une maison ouverte, tout en la protégeant de l'inclémence du vent qui fouette cette zone. La forme de la parcelle a influencé la conception triangulaire du plan qui distribue la zone noble, le jardin et la piscine vers le sud pour les protéger du vent et les orienter vers le splendide panorama sur la mer et la baie de Cadaqués. Peu élevée au-dessus du sol, cette construction, utilisant des matériaux comme la pierre locale, le verre et l'aluminium anodisé, se fond harmonieusement dans le paysage côtier, au sein d'un jardin planté d'oliviers et de cyprès.

Für die Planung dieses Hauses an einer Steilküste der wilden Costa Brava war die wundervolle Lage des Grundstücks inmitten der Natur und dessen eigentümliche dreieckige Form von Anfang an entscheidend. Der außergewöhnliche Standort, mit dem Meer gegenüber, und der weite Blick über die Landschaft machten es unerlässlich, ein offenes Haus zu schaffen, wenn es auch gegen den starken Wind, der in dieser Region weht, geschützt werden musste. Mit einem dreieckigen Grundriss folgte man der eigentümlichen Form des Grundstücks, so dass im Süden ein privilegierter Bereich mit Garten und Swimmingpool entstand, der vor Winden geschützt ist und einen wundervollen Panoramablick auf das Meer und die Bucht von Cadaqués bietet. Das Haus fügt sich harmonisch in die Küstenlandschaft ein, weil es flach und aus Natursteinen der Region gebaut wurde, Glas und eloxiertes Aluminium benutzt wurde und weil es von einem Garten voller Olivenbäume und Zypressen umgeben ist.

The unbeatable location facing the sea was exploited to build a house totally open to the majestic landscape of the Costa Brava.

L'incomparable emplacement face à la mer invitait à concevoir une habitation complètement ouverte sur le majestueux paysage de la Costa Brava.

Dieser wundervolle Standort direkt am Meer führte dazu, ein völlig offenes Haus zu planen, von dem aus man die majestädische Landschaft der Costa Brava überschaut.

Ugarte House

Maison Ugarte

Haus Ugarte

This weekend getaway with subtle lines and extremely luminous spaces is situated some 80 miles north of Santiago. Its simple structure reflects the traditional buildings in the region, especially in the wood cladding of the stark, untreated façades, which gives the house the air of a mountain cabin. Wooden planks were also used inside the house to cover both the floors and the walls. The color of the wood is echoed in the furnishings, although some pieces, such as the lampshades, break up the uniformity of the ocher color scheme. The roof on top of the building adds a light touch, especially when seen with the Pacific Ocean as a backdrop; when the house is observed from the opposite angle, however, facing away from the sea, it stands out as an attractive structure that redefines and reinterprets the surrounding countryside.

Ce refuge de week-end aux lignes subtiles, doté d'espaces extrêmement lumineux, est situé à 130 km au nord de Santiago. La simplicité de sa structure rappelle les constructions plus traditionnelles de la région, spécialement dans le bois qui couvre toutes les façades, d'aspect brut et non traité, qui confère à la maison une apparence de refuge de montagne. La toiture qui coiffe la construction semble toute légère, surtout avec l'océan Pacifique en toile de fond. Toutefois, vue de l'angle opposé, loin de la mer, la résidence se métamorphose en une structure attractive qui redéfinit et réinterprète la campagne environnante. A l'intérieur aussi, on a choisi des lattes de bois, qui tapissent à la fois les sols et les murs. Les tons de bois se retrouvent dans le mobilier, même si certains éléments, comme les lampes, rompent l'uniformité chromatique des tons ocre.

Dieses Wochenendhaus mit feinen Linien und sehr hellen Räumen befindet sich 130 km nördlich von Santiago. Die einfache Struktur imitiert die traditionellen Bauten der Region, wozu auch die Verwendung von rohem, unbehandeltem Holz beiträgt, mit dem alle Fassaden verkleidet sind. So wirkt das Haus wie eine Berghütte. Das Dach, welches das Gebäude krönt, hat eine sehr leichte Struktur, eine Leichtigkeit, die durch den Pazifischen Ozean im Hintergrund noch verstärkt wird. Wenn man es jedoch von einer anderen Seite betrachtet, etwas weiter vom Meer entfernt, hat es eine ansprechende Form, die das umgebende Ackerland neu definiert und interpretiert. Im Inneren wurden Holztafeln verbaut, die sowohl Böden als auch die Wände bedecken. Die Farbe des Holzes wird auch bei den Möbeln beibehalten, obwohl es einige Elemente gibt, wie z.B. die Lampenschirme, die diese farbliche Einheitlichkeit mit Ockertönen unterbrechen.

The interplay of volumes marks out a clear and concise alternation that sets up a dialogue between the concepts of fullness and void.

Le jeu de volumes définit une claire et précise alternance géométrique dans un dialogue entre le plein et le vide.

Das Spiel mit den Formen definiert den Wechsel der klaren und genauen Geometrie, in der ein Dialog zwischen den Konzepten Fülle und Leere stattfindet.

The building substantially alters the landscape and thereby reinterprets it.

La construction modifie considérablement le paysage, dans le sens d'une transformation et d'une réinterprétation.

Das Gebäude verändert die Landschaft relativ stark, es formt sie um und interpretiert sie neu.

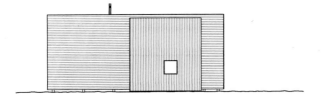

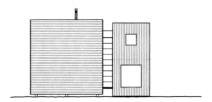

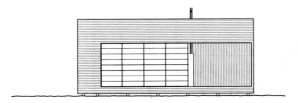

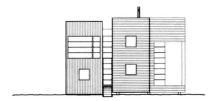

› Elevations Élévations Aufrisse

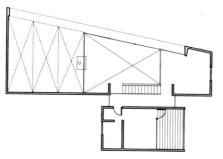

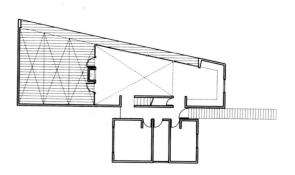

› Plans Plans Grundrisse

66

House in Eastern View

Maison à Eastern View

Haus in Eastern View

This site in Victoria is exposed to extremely cold storms blown in from Antarctica during the winter, while summer can be characterized by long hot days on the beach and cool winds in the afternoon, tainted only by the ever present threat of bushfire. The client wanted to have a home that provided balance, capitalizing on the powerful natural environment and forces in which the site indulges. In contrast to much of the housing built in prominent locations, this house does not perform structural gymnastics to maximize views in a resulting obtrusive form. Rather, the structure falls behind the primary dune and follows the natural gradient of the sloping terrain. Shielded at the back by a state forest, the house is invisible from passing traffic, offering privacy and seclusion.

Cet endroit de l'état de Victoria est exposé durant l'hiver à des tempêtes extrêmement froides provenant de l'Antarctique. L'été, en revanche, les journées sont longues et chaudes, accompagnées de vents chauds au crépuscule, que seule la sempiternelle menace d'incendie peut assombrir. Le client souhaitait avoir une demeure harmonieuse où se ressourcer en tirant le meilleur parti de l'impressionnant environnement naturel. Contrastant avec de nombreuses habitations placées à de tels endroits, cette maison n'utilise pas de structures audacieuses pour optimaliser ses vues. La structure est plutôt mise en retrait derrière une dune, se fondant à la pente naturelle du terrain incliné. Protégée à l'arrière par un bois public, la maison ainsi à l'abri de l'activité urbaine, gagne en intimité et isolement.

Dieser Ort im Staat Victoria ist den ganzen Winter über kalten Stürmen ausgesetzt, die aus der Antarktis kommen. Im Sommer hingegen sind die Tage lang und heiß und morgens wehen warme Winde, wobei jedoch ständig Brandgefahr besteht. Der Kunde wünschte sich ein Haus, das mit sich selbst und mit der umgebenden Natur im Gleichgewicht ist. Im Gegensatz zu vielen Häusern an ähnlichen Standorten verwendete man für dieses Haus nicht die strukturellen Tricks, die die Aussicht verbessern. Stattdessen verbirgt sich die Struktur hinter einer Düne und nutzt die natürliche Neigung des Bodens aus. Von hinten wird es von einem öffentlichen Wald geschützt, so dass das Haus für den Durchgangsverkehr unsichtbar wird und viel Privatsphäre und Isolation bietet.

The mass of trees to the rear of the house leaves it semi-hidden from passersby, thereby achieving the privacy seecked by the client.

Grâce à un massif arboré accolé à la partie arrière, l'habitation est partiellement à l'abri des regards indiscrets, répondant ainsi au désir d'intimité du client.

Ein kleiner Baumbestand hinter dem Haus verbirgt das Gebäude vor den Blicken der Passanten und schützt die Privatsphäre.

› Elevations Élévations Aufrisse

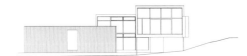

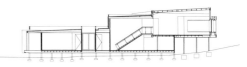

› Section Section Schnitt

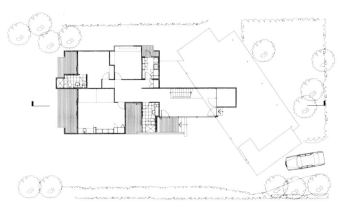

› Ground floor Rez-de-chaussée Erdgeschoss

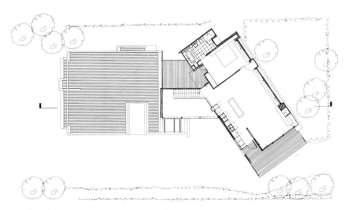

› First floor Premier étage Erstes Obergeschoss

A meticulously designed system of adjustable shutters makes it possible to regulate the amount of sunlight that penetrates into the interior.

Un système bien étudié de stores réglables permet de contrôler l'intensité de la lumière solaire qui pénètre à l'intérieur.

Ein ausgeklügeltes System verstellbarer Jalousien macht es möglich, die Menge an Sonnenlicht, die ins Innere fällt, zu steuern.

House on the Seashore

Maison au bord de la mer

Haus am Meeresrand

The thick tree cover on this lot led the architects to raise the house's main structure to take advantage of this feature and integrate the principal rooms into the surrounding vegetation. A steel frame reinforces the wooden structure and supports the large projections that heighten the relationship with the environment. As the upper levels were reserved for the daytime areas and the bedrooms, the bottom floor became the ideal place for installing a guest bedroom, study and private gym, as well as a storage room. A large shower was installed next to the gym; it is clad entirely with wood, although it receives natural light through slats that are set sufficiently far apart to also provide ventilation. The sober colors used in the interior establish a strong contrast with the appearance of the house when seen from the outside.

La grande densité boisée de ce terrain a conduit les architectes à élever la structure principale de cette maison et en profiter pour intégrer les pièces principales à la végétation environnante. Un châssis d'acier renforce la structure de bois et soutient les grands angles saillants qui exaltent la relation avec l'environnement. En réservant la zone de jour et les chambres à coucher sur les niveaux supérieurs, le rez-de-chaussée s'est transformé en lieu idéal pour abriter une chambre d'amis, un studio et une salle de gymnastique privée, ainsi qu'un espace de rangement. A côté de la salle de gymnastique, on a installé une grande douche entièrement lambrissée qui reçoit la lumière naturelle grâce à un système de lames suffisamment séparées entre elles pour également favoriser l'aération. La palette de tons sobres utilisée à l'intérieur crée un violent contraste avec l'aspect de l'habitation vue de l'extérieur.

Der dichte Baumbestand auf dem Grundstück brachte die Architekten auf die Idee, die Hauptstruktur dieses Hauses zu erhöhen und die Bäume zu nutzen, um die wichtigsten Räume in die umgebende Vegetation miteinzubeziehen. Ein Stahlrahmen verstärkt die Holzstruktur und stützt die großen Auskragungen, die die Beziehung zur Umgebung betonen. Da sich die tagsüber genutzten Räume und die Schlafzimmer auf den oberen Etagen befinden, stellte das Erdgeschoss den idealen Ort für das Gästezimmer und ein privates Fitnessstudio dar. Ebenso gibt es hier Lagerräume. Neben dem Fitnessraum befindet sich eine vollständig mit Holz verkleidete Dusche, die mit Tafeln umgeben ist, zwischen denen genug Abstand ist, um Licht und Luft durchzulassen. Die in den Räumen verwendeten Farben sind relativ zurückhaltend, was zu einem starken Kontrast mit dem äußeren Erscheinungsbild dieses Hauses führt.

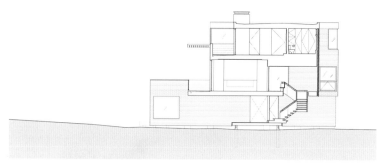

› Longitudinal section Section longitudinale Längsschnitt

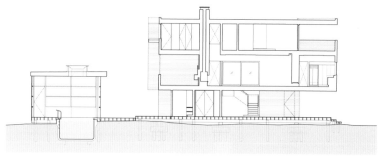

› Cross section Section transversale Querschnitt

Natural light penetrates every nook and cranny of the house, even the shower in the gym.

La lumière naturelle fénètre dans tous les coins de la maison, même jusqu'à la douche de la salle de gymnastique.

Das Tageslicht erreicht auch die letzten Winkel des Hauses, sogar die Dusche im Sportstudio.

The sober color scheme used in the interior establishes a strong contrast with the external appearance of the home.

La palette de tons sobres employée à l'intérieur contraste fortement avec l'aspect extérieur de l'habitation.

Die in den Räumen verwendeten Farben sind relativ zurückhaltend, was zu einem starken Kontrast mit dem äußeren Erscheinungsbild dieses Hauses führt.

Reyna Residence

Résidence Reyna

Haus Reyna

This residence, which is forever interacting with the exterior and at the same time protective of its private life, looks toward the peninsula of Palos Verdes and the island of Santa Catalina from Hermosa beach. Its changing environment is formed by extremely old and small constructions together with contemporary buildings with great architectural importance. The layout of the house is organized in a vertical sequence of three levels, which ascend toward the most private space. A guest room, family room and parking are located on the ground floor next to the double entrance. The living room, dining room and kitchen occupy the two intermediate levels, while the master bedroom and bathroom are located on the top floor to take advantage of the best views. Each one of the three floors extends to the exterior with terraces that overlook the oceanfront to provide magnificent views.

Cette résidence, conjuguant une constante interaction avec l'extérieur et une protection jalouse de la vie privée, est tournée vers la péninsule de Palos Verdes et l'île de Santa Catalina, depuis la plage Hermosa. Elle s'inscrit dans un environnement parsemé d'anciennes petites maisons entre lesquelles surgissent des édifices modernes d'une valeur architecturale certaine. La conception de l'habitation s'organise autour d'une séquence verticale, développée sur trois niveaux. Le rez-de-chaussée accueille, à côté d'une vaste entrée, une chambre d'amis, une salle et le garage. Le salon, la salle à manger et la cuisine occupent les deux niveaux intermédiaires. La chambre à coucher des propriétaires et la salle de bains sont à l'étage supérieur, profitant ainsi des plus belles vues. Les trois étages s'ouvrent sur l'extérieur avec des terrasses qui donnent sur la mer, permettant de jouir d'un paysage magnifique.

Dieses Haus, das in einer ewig währenden Beziehung zur Umgebung steht und gleichzeitig die Intimsphäre seiner Bewohner behütet, blickt vom Strand Playa Hermosa in Richtung der Halbinsel Palos Verdes und der Insel Santa Catalina. In seiner Nachbarschaft befinden sich verschiedene kleine, alte Häuser, unter denen sich vereinzelt moderne Gebäude von beachtlichem, architektonischem Interesse erheben. Das Gebäude ist vertikal auf drei Ebenen organisiert. Im Untergeschoss, in der Nähe des Eingangs, befinden sich das Gästezimmer, ein Saal und die Garage. Das Wohnzimmer, das Speisezimmer und die Küche nehmen die beiden Zwischengeschosse ein. Das Hauptschlafzimmer und das Bad liegen im Obergeschoss, so dass man von hier aus den besten Ausblick auf die landschaftlich sehr schöne Umgebung hat. Die drei Etagen öffnen sich über die Terrassen, die zum Meer liegen, nach außen, so dass man die wundervolle Landschaft genießen kann.

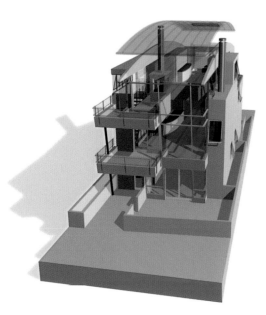

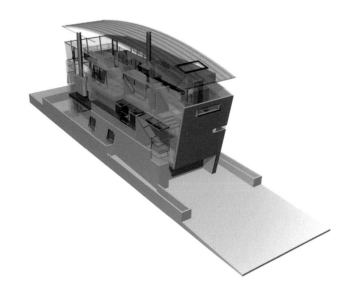

› Perspectives Perspectives Perspektivzeichnungen

The domestic program is organized in a vertical sequence of three levels, all open to the exterior by means of terraces that give on to the sea.

Le programme domestique s'organise autour d'une séquence verticale sur trois niveaux, tous ouverts sur l'extérieur par le biais de terrasses qui donnent sur la mer.

Die gesamten notwendigen Wohnräume sind vertikal über drei Ebenen verteilt, und alle öffnen sich über die Terrassen zum Meer.

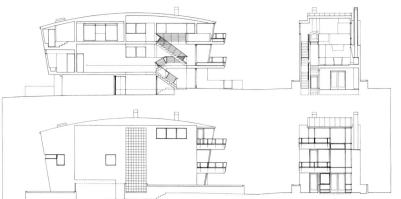

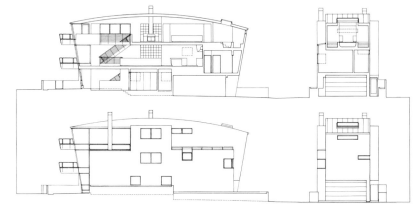

› Elevations Élévations Aufrisse

Residence in Capistrano Beach
Résidence sur la plage Capistrano
Haus am Strand Capistrano

The residences built at Capistrano Beach in recent years represent the typical condition of the beach front in southern California: increased crowding. Such is the case with this house, which makes the most of its surroundings and the available surface area. The interior features so much glass and light that the walls seem nonexistent and the materials seem to disappear. The architectural challenge was to maximize the space, the presence of the beach and the spectacular views of the landscape. The architect's solution was to create a large, curved wall, which is used as a reference throughout the project. The wall establishes appropriate degrees of privacy and contrasts with the rigid and orthogonal geometry of the land. Despite the site's minimal proportions the architect created interesting areas and paths. The result is a project of multiple spatial relationships that continually offers new sensations.

L'architecture érigée ces dernières années sur la plage Capistrano, affiche les caractéristiques du front de mer du sud de la Californie, marqué par une urbanisation en croissance constante. Cette demeure vise à embrasser un maximum de surface extérieure, alors que l'intérieur se présente comme un objet dématérialisé, par le biais de l'action de la lumière et de l'espace. L'architecte s'est vu face au défi d'exploiter à la fois la présence de la plage et les vues panoramiques. A cet effet, le choix s'est porté sur la construction d'un grand mur incurvé, point de référence de tout le projet, établissant les degrés d'intimité adéquats, tout en contrastant avec la géométrie rigoureuse et carrée de la propriété. Malgré les dimensions réduites du terrain, les espaces et les déplacements sont intéressants. Le projet final offre des relations spatiales multiples avec, à la clé, la découverte constante d'effets surprenants.

Die Gebäude, die in den letzten Jahren am Strand Capistrano errichtet wurden, sind typisch für die Architektur an der südkalifornischen Küste, die immer dichter besiedelt wird. Während das Gebäude von außen so viel Platz wie möglich einnimmt, wirkt es im Inneren durch die Art und Weise, wie das Licht und der Raum benutzt werden, wie eine Art immaterielles Objekt. Die Herausforderung, der sich der Architekt stellte, bestand darin, den nahe liegenden Strand und den wundervollen Ausblick in die Planung zu integrieren. Dazu schuf er eine große gebogene Mauer, die als Referenz für das gesamte Gebäude dient. Diese Mauer sorgt für genügend Privatsphäre und bildet gleichzeitig einen Gegensatz zu der strengen und quadratischen Form des Grundstücks. Obwohl das Gelände nicht besonders groß ist, schuf man interessante Räume und Wege. Das Ergebnis ist ein Haus voller verschiedener räumlicher Beziehungen, in dem man ständig etwas Neues entdecken kann.

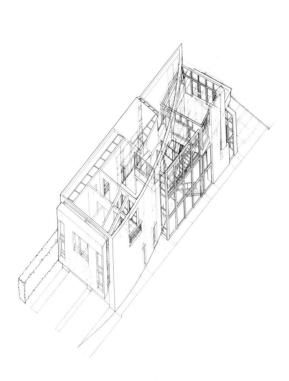

› **Perspective** Perspective Perspektivzeichnung

Residence in Uruguay

Résidence à Uruguay

Haus in Uruguay

This house is set on an 820-ft-high cliff that is lashed by winds every day from noon onward. On the one hand, the beauty of the landscape cried out for transparency, but, on the other, the harshness of the climatic conditions demanded a solid construction that would be unperturbed by the howling gales. In response to these two pre-conditions, a stone and glass block consisting of stacked prismatic volumes was designed. Its L-shape protects the porch and swimming pool from the wind and makes it possible to enjoy the view not only from every room but also from the patio, via the windows that enclose most of the perimeter. Due to the erosive impact of the incessant wind and sea, highly resistant materials such as gray granite and exposed concrete were used on the lintels, staircases, floors and swimming pool.

Cette demeure, située en haut d'une falaise à 250 m d'altitude, est de ce fait quotidiennement exposée aux caprices du vent. D'un côté, la beauté du paysage imposait la recherche de transparence, mais de l'autre, la dureté des conditions climatiques exigeait la conception d'une construction qui puisse résister aux assauts des ouragans. Face à ces deux exigences, la solution a été de concevoir un bloc de pierre et de verre sous forme de volumes prismatiques empilés l'un sur l'autre. La conception en L protège l'entrée et la piscine du vent et permet de jouir des vues depuis toutes les pièces et même depuis le patio, grâce aux baies vitrées qui s'étirent sur une bonne partie du périmètre. Pour pallier la forte érosion du vent constant, on a recouru à des matériaux extrêmement résistants, comme le granit gris et le béton apparent du plafond, des linteaux, des escaliers, des sols et de la piscine.

Dieses Haus steht auf einer 250 m hohen Steilküste und ist jeden Tag starken Winden ausgesetzt. Aufgrund der Schönheit der Landschaft suchte man einerseits nach Transparenz, andererseits war man durch die harten klimatischen Bedingungen dazu gezwungen, ein solides Haus zu errichten, das den Winden gleichmütig trotzt. Als Lösung für diese beiden Bestrebungen wurde ein Block aus Stein und Glas in prismenförmigen, gestapelten Abschnitten entworfen. Seine L-Form schützt die Terrasse und den Swimmingpool vor dem Wind und gibt den Blick aus allen Räumen und sogar vom Hof durch die großen Fenster frei, die einen großen Teil der Fassade einnehmen. Um der unaufhörlichen Erosionskraft des Windes zu trotzen, verwendete man sehr widerstandsfähige Materialien wie graues Granitgestein und polierten Beton in den Außenbereichen, an den Fenster- und Türstürzen, den Böden und dem Swimmingpool.

Some of the furniture, such as the orange couch and table, create a vivid contrast with the pale colors of the white walls.

Certains meubles comme le divan et la table oranges créent un contraste vif avec les tons clairs des murs blancs.

Die Fenster der Küche ermöglichen eine gute Belüftung und machen das Gebäude transparent.

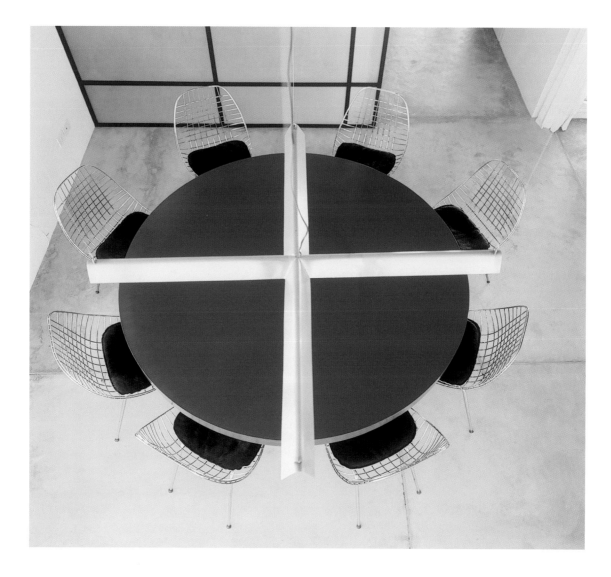

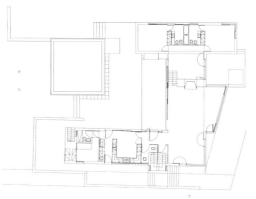

› Ground floor   Rez-de-chaussée   Erdgeschoss

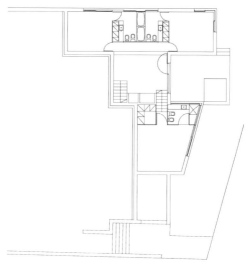

› First floor   Premier étage   Erstes Obergeschoss

Rochman Residence

Résidence Rochman

Rochman Haus

This refurbished 1950s' house, situated on a hillside in Pacific Palisades, enjoys panoramic views of the coasts of Santa Monica and Malibu. It is spread over 3,000 sq. ft and appears to be a single-story building from the front entrance, although it is obvious from the rear that there are in fact two floors. Restrictions on height and the need for distance from other houses led the roof to be designed as a continuous horizontal parapet shared with the outer walls, which tilt outward from the center of the house, thereby heightening the sense of spaciousness inside. From below, the building resembles a two-story wedge, inserted into the slope and jutting out toward the sea. An orange plaster wall running along the entrance marks out the transversal axis and divides the private area on the lower level from the public space on the top floor.

Située au bord d'une colline des Pacific Palisades, cette maison des années cinquante, restaurée, bénéficie de vues panoramiques sur la côte de Santa Monica et Malibu. La maison, de 280 m², se présente, dès l'entrée, comme une demeure d'un seul niveau, pour dévoiler ensuite l'existence de deux étages sur la partie arrière. Les réglementations limitant la hauteur et les distances entre les maisons font que la toiture est conçue à l'instar d'un parapet horizontal continu, coupé par les murs externes qui se penchent vers l'extérieur à partir du centre de la maison pour exalter la sensation d'espace à l'intérieur. Vu d'en bas, l'édifice ressemble à une cale cunéiforme de deux étages, insérée sur le terrain incliné qui surplombe la mer depuis la colline. Un mur de plâtre orangé, le long de l'entrée, définit l'axe transversal et deux zones, une privée au niveau inférieur et une publique à l'étage.

Dieses Haus am Rande einer Anhöhe in Pacific Palisades stammt ursprünglich aus den Fünfzigerjahren und bietet einen wundervollen Rundblick auf die Küsten von Santa Monica und Malibu. Das 280 m² große Haus sieht auf den ersten Blick einstöckig aus. Beim Betreten erkennt man jedoch, dass es im hinteren Teil zwei Etagen hat. Da es für die Höhe und den Abstand zu den anderen Häusern strenge Bauvorschriften gibt, wurde das Dach wie eine durchgehende waagerechte Brüstung entworfen, die die Mauern einschließt. Die Mauern neigen sich vom Inneren des Hauses nach außen, wodurch der Eindruck von Weite in den Räumen verstärkt wird. Von unten gesehen gleicht das Gebäude einem zweistöckigen Keil, der in ein geneigtes Gelände eingefügt ist und aus der Anhöhe in Richtung Meer hinausragt. Eine mit orangefarbenem Gips verputzte Wand am Eingang definiert die Querachse und trennt die privaten Räume im Untergeschoss von den öffentlichen im Obergeschoss.

Exposed concrete is the dominant material outside, both on the façade and on the roof.

Le béton apparent est le matériau omniprésent à l'extérieur, tant sur la façade que sur la toiture.

Unverputzter Beton ist das vorherrschende Material im Freien, sowohl an der Fassade als auch am Dach.

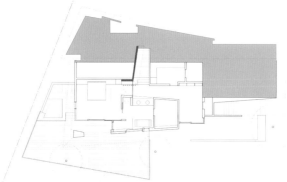

› **Ground floor** Rez-de-chaussée Erdgeschoss

› **First floor** Premier étage Erstes Obergeschoss

A roof made of cedar-wood beams extends beyond the dining room to make the terrace more comfortable on hot summer days.

Une toiture en poutres de cèdre, qui s'étend au-delà de la salle à manger, rend la terrasse plus habitable les jours où le rayonnement solaire est particulièrement fort.

Eine Decke aus Zedernbalken ragt aus dem Speisezimmer heraus und macht so die Terrasse an Tagen mit starker Sonne bewohnbarer.

Yallingup Residence
Résidence Yallingup
Residenz Yallingup

The sloping lot on which this residence is located affords the residents stunning views of the Indian Ocean. The project's objective was twofold: to adapt the building to the irregularities of the land and to maintain a balanced vision of the overall construction. The home's design—in a solid and linear architecture—is a departure from the typical wooden houses of the village. The steel structure of the house was softened by a curved roof and wooden screens that elevate the volume on the side of the hill. The house's rectangular form is unified by terraces with projections that break the curved roofline of the principal volume. The two floors of the residence feature glass windows and spacious terraces that make the most of the stunning views.

Le terrain en pente, accueillant cette résidence, permet de bénéficier de vues sur l'océan Indien. La construction devait s'adapter aux irrégularités du sol, tout en préservant une vision d'ensemble harmonieuse. En outre, l'architecte devait s'éloigner du style traditionnel de maisons de bois pour trouver une solution plus solide et linéaire. La structure d'acier a gardé sa légèreté avec la couverture du toit et les écrans de bois qui élèvent le volume en douceur. La forme rectangulaire de l'ensemble a gardé son unité après avoir couvert les terrasses d'un encorbellement rompant avec la courbe de la toiture du volume principal. Pour profiter des vues sur le paysage environnant, les deux étages de la résidence disposent de baies vitrées et de vastes terrasses sur tout le pourtour.

Da dieses Haus auf einem Abhang steht, hat man einen wundervollen Blick auf den Indischen Ozean. Das Haus musste an die Unebenheiten des Geländes angepasst werden und dennoch einen harmonischen Anblick bieten. Außerdem war es der Wunsch der Eigentümer, nicht dem traditionellen Stil der Holzhäuser zu folgen, sondern auf eine andere Art eine stabile und lineare Lösung zu finden. Die Stahlstruktur wirkt durch die Biegung des Daches und die Holzschirme, die das Gebäude auf sanfte Art erhöhen, weniger schwer. Die rechteckige Form des gesamten Gebäudes wurde durch das Dach der Terrasse vereinheitlicht, dessen Vorsprung die Kurvenform des Daches des Hauptgebäudes unterbricht. Um die wundervolle Aussicht auf die umgebende Natur auszunutzen, gibt es in beiden Stockwerken überall große Fenster und Terrassen.

The substantial terraces around the house establish a strong link between the architecture and the surroundings.

Les importantes terrasses qui entourent la maison créent un lien étroit entre l'architecture et l'environnement où la demeure est implantée.

Die großen Terrassen, die das Haus umgeben, schaffen eine starke Verbindung zwischen der Architektur und der Landschaft, in der sich das Haus befindet.

Raising the building above the height of the vegetation and integrating it into the terrain allows both levels to enjoy views of the sea.

L'idée d'élever la construction pour préserver la hauteur de la végétation et l'intégrer au terrain, permet à ses deux étages de bénéficier des vues sur la mer.

Durch die erhöhte Lage des Hauses, hat man von den beiden Etagen aus einen sehr schönen Blick auf das Meer.

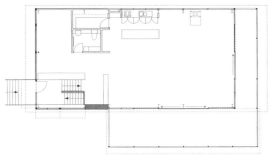

› Ground floor   Rez-de-chaussée   Erdgeschoss

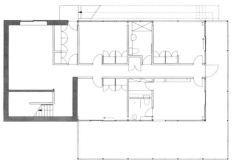

› First floor   Premier étage   Erstes Obergeschoss

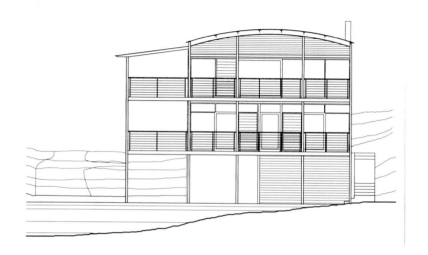

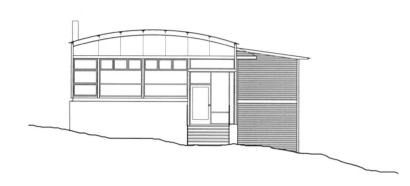

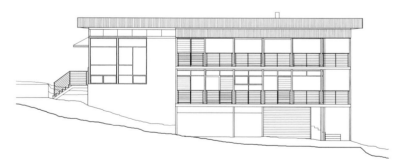

› Elevations Élévations Aufrisse

House in Dirk Bay

Maison à baie Dirk

Haus in Bucht Dirk

In the shelter of a small cape near the Galley Head lighthouse, a house was built years ago for the coastguard, and its placement guaranteed the success of many a rescue mission. The project involved refurbishing this robust house—situated by a ramp leading to the sea—and its hangar, as well as adding a new building. The three volumes are linked by an asymmetrical cross-shape cloister that provides the garden in the courtyard leading to the beach with protection from the wind. The need to shelter the old house from the inclement weather had caused it to be built facing south-southeast, but this reduced the hours in which it was exposed to sunlight. As the sun is a precious commodity in Ireland, the new volume was designed to capture the very last rays of the setting sun by placing it on an outcrop that juts towards the sea, out of reach of the shadows of the neighboring hills.

Non loin du phare de Galley Head, la maison du garde-côtes a été construite autrefois en plein vent au bord d'un petit cap, emplacement idéal pour assurer les sauvetages en mer. Le projet visait à restaurer cette maison solide, construite sur la rampe d'accès à la mer, ainsi que le claustra cruciforme asymétrique, agissant en pare vent pour le patio paysagé qui permet d'accéder à la plage. Autrefois, pour protéger l'ancienne bâtisse des intempéries, on a opté pour une orientation est sud-est, diminuant les heures d'ensoleillement. Vu l'importance de la lumière naturelle dans cette zone, le nouveau volume a été conçu pour capter les derniers rayons de soleil couchant. D'où la nouvelle implantation sur un encorbellement qui s'avance vers la mer, s'éloignant ainsi de l'ombre des collines environnantes.

Dieses solide Haus, das man auf einer Zugangsrampe zum Meer und einer Halle errichtete, wurde renoviert und ein neues Gebäude konstruiert. Die drei Gebäudeteile sind durch einen kreuzförmigen und asymmetrischen Kreuzgang miteinander verbunden, der die Winde von dem begrünten Hof, den man vom Strand aus betritt, abhält. In der Vergangenheit war es notwendig, das Haus vor dem Wetter zu schützen, deshalb wählte man eine Ost-Süd-Ost Ausrichtung, durch die auch die Zeit der Sonneneinwirkung verringert wurde. Da das Tageslicht in dieser Region jedoch sehr wertvoll ist, hat man den neuen Anbau so geplant, dass auch die letzten Strahlen der untergehenden Sonne eingefangen werden. Deshalb liegt es auf einem Vorsprung, der ins Meer hinausragt und sich vom Schatten der umgebenden Anhöhen entfernt.

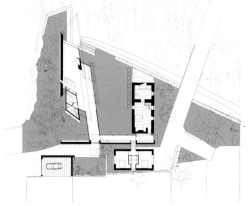

› Location plan   Plan de situation   Umgebungsplan

The design of the new volume aims to capture as much daylight as possible, hence the predominance of glass and the color white.

La conception de la nouvelle construction obéit à la nécessité de capter les derniers rayons du soleil du jour, ce qui explique la prédominance du verre et de la couleur blanche.

Mit der Gestaltung des neuen Anbaus sollten die letzten Sonnenstrahlen des Tages eingefangen werden. Deshalb wurde Glas und die Farbe Weiß verwendet.

James Robertson House

Maison James Robertson

James Robertson Haus

The topography of the terrain, situated in an idyllic bay on the east coast of Australia—a slope going straight from the beach up to the edge of a cliff—decisively determined this home's architectural configuration. In order to integrate it into the rugged environment, it was decided to build two pavilions that would be surrounded by trees and rocks, so that sun, shade, views and privacy would all be obtained from strictly natural sources. The house is reached from the sea, by means of a ferry linking Great Mackeral Beach with the nearest town. From this beach, a path leads up to the imposing sandstone retaining wall dug into the slope to mark off the first pavilion, shrouded with bamboo, with its studio, guest room and larder. The path continues along copper-clad walls to the double-height main space, which contains the communal areas.

Cette résidence est implantée sur un terrain à flanc de coteau, s'élevant de la plage même jusqu'au bord d'une falaise qui surplombe une baie paradisiaque de la côte est australienne. Sa topographie particulière a été déterminante dans la coupe architecturale de la demeure. Afin de l'insérer dans cet environnement escarpé, on a construit deux pavillons entourés d'arbres et de rochers, bénéficiant à la fois de lumière, de panoramas et d'intimité. L'accès à l'habitation se fait par la mer grâce à une navette qui relie la plage Great Mackeral au village le plus proche. Un chemin part de cette plage vers l'imposant mur de soutènement en grès, creusé dans le coteau qui délimite le premier pavillon où les bambous entourent le studio, la chambre d'amis et la réserve. Le sentier continue à côté des murs revêtus de cuivre de l'espace principal, à double hauteur, qui abrite les zones communes.

Das Grundstück liegt auf einem Abhang, der sich vom Strand bis zu einer Steilküste erstreckt, von der aus man auf eine paradiesische Bucht an der australischen Ostküste schaut. Die besondere Bodenform hat die architektonische Aufteilung des Hauses deutlich bestimmt. Um das Haus in die schroffe Umgebung zu integrieren und die Privatsphäre der Bewohner zu schützen, wurden zwei Flügel errichtet. Die beiden Flügel sind sehr hell und der Ausblick ist wundervoll. Man erreicht das Haus vom Meer mit einer Fähre, über den Strand Great Mackeral. Vom Strand aus führt ein Weg zu der gewaltigen Umfassungsmauer aus Sandstein, der aus einem nahegelegenen Steinbruch stammt. Diese Mauer begrenzt den ersten Flügel, in dem Bambussträucher das Arbeitszimmer, das Gästezimmer und die Speisekammer umgeben. Der Pfad führt vorbei an den mit Kupfer verkleideten Mauern zu dem wichtigsten Gebäudeteil doppelter Höhe, in dem sich die gemeinsam bewohnten Bereiche befinden.

The house is reached from the sea, by means of a boat that links Great Mackerel Beach with the nearest town.

L'accès à la demeure s'effectue par mer, grâce à une navette qui relie la plage Great Mackeral au village le plus proche.

Der Zugang zum Haus erfolgt vom Meer aus über eine Fähre, die den Strand Great Mackeral mit dem nächsten Ort verbindet.

› Ground floor Rez-de-chaussée Erdgeschoss

› First floor Premier étage Erstes Obergeschoss

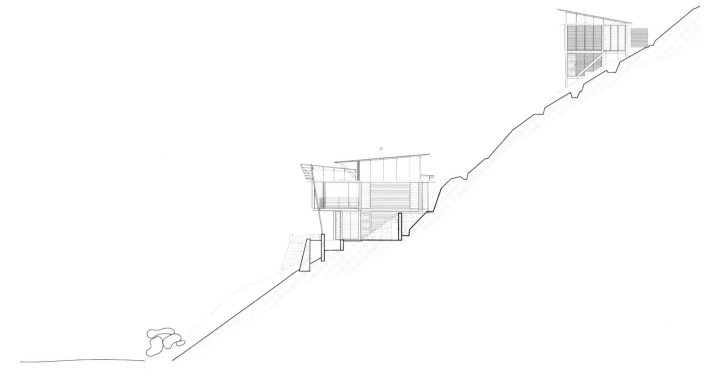

› Longitudinal section Section longitudinale Längsschnitt

House in Port Fairy

Maison à Port Fairy

Haus in Port Fairy

This house, a mere 165 feet from the seashore, is tucked between dunes and thickets of tea trees. This setting provides many opportunities for outdoor activities, and the house is designed to protect its occupants from the wind while allowing in plenty of sunlight. Simplicity and purity were the watchwords for the construction, despite its relatively large scale. The building, set on a base of plastered brickwork and clad with strips of painted eucalyptus, uses unconventional spaces that are in constant transition. The outdoor areas are enclosed by the structure of the building, while the upper terrace is fully exterior, even though it is designed in the same way as the interior spaces. The terrace provides 360-degree views of a picturesque fishing village, complete with huge Norfolk pines and blue stone buildings.

Cette habitation se love entre les dunes et les buissons de théiers, à 50 m à peine du rivage. Vu les nombreuses possibilités d'activités extérieures, la maison est conçue pour protéger ses habitants du vent tout en laissant passer la lumière solaire. Pureté et simplicité inspirent les formes de cette construction, très spacieuse. L'édifice, revêtu de lattes de bois d'eucalyptus peintes, posé sur un socle de briques enduites de plâtre, offre des espaces non conventionnels, en mouvement constant. La forme de l'édifice définit les espaces extérieurs. La terrasse supérieure, entièrement à l'extérieur, suit le même schéma que les espaces intérieurs. Celle-ci offre une vue panoramique de 360° sur le pittoresque village de pêcheurs avec ses immenses pins de Norfolk et ses bâtiments en pierre bleue.

Dieses Haus liegt nur 50 m vom Meeresufer entfernt, sehr geschützt zwischen Dünen und Teebäumen. Da es viele Möglichkeiten gibt, einer Beschäftigung unter freiem Himmel nachzugehen, ist das Haus so gestaltet, dass seine Bewohner vom Wind geschützt sind und reichlich Sonnenlicht einfällt. Die Architektur ist maßgeblich von Reinheit und Einfachheit inspiriert. Das Gebäude ist mit Platten aus lackiertem Eukalyptusholz verkleidet und ruht auf einem Fundament aus verputztem Ziegel. Die Räume sind sehr unkonventionell gestaltet und befinden sich in ständigem Übergang. Die Außenbereiche werden durch die Form des Gebäudes geschützt. Die obere Terrasse liegt völlig im Freien, obwohl sie wie ein Innenraum gestaltet ist. Von der Terrasse aus hat man einen wundervollen Rundblick auf das malerische Fischerdorf mit seinen riesigen Norfolk-Pinien und Gebäuden aus blauem Stein.

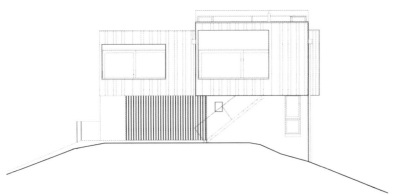

› North elevation Élévation nord Nördlicher Aufriss

› East elevation Élévation est Östlicher Aufriss

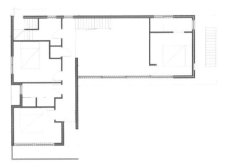

› Ground floor Rez-de-chaussée Erdgeschoss

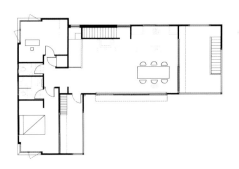

› First floor Premier étage Erstes Obergeschoss

The landscape penetrates into the daytime areas to become another decorative element, even in the kitchen.

Le paysage pénètre dans les zones de jour pour se transformer en un élément décoratif supplémentaire, y compris dans la cuisine.

Die Landschaft dringt in die tagsüber bewohnten Bereiche ein und wird so zu einem weiteren Dekorationselement, sogar in der Küche.

House in Cascais

Maison à Cascais

Haus in Cascais

Souto de Moura's style hardly needs any introduction—all lovers of architecture are familiar with his passion for precision and utmost sensitivity to the context. This house in Cascais consolidates still further this Portuguese architect's reputation for rationalism, but he adds a touch of warmth to this approach through the choice of materials and the adoption of local building traditions. The house is structured around a lower ground floor containing the service facilities that serves as the base for the main volume, set perpendicular to the gradient and thus requiring concrete pillars as supports. The interior layout establishes a clear spatial division between the daytime and night-time areas; the two are separated by the staircase leading to the lower floor, which can also be reached directly from the exterior due to the lay of the land.

Inutile de présenter le style de Souto de Moura : les amoureux de l'architecture connaissent sa passion pour la précision et son extrême sensibilité pour l'environnement. Cette maison située à Cascais renforce une fois de plus le parcours rationaliste de l'architecte portugais, avec en plus une touche chaleureuse ajoutée à sa conception des matériaux et à l'approche de la tradition en matière de construction locale. La maison s'appuie sur un demi sous-sol qui accueille les services et fait office de socle pour le volume principal. La position particulière de ce volume – perpendiculaire à la pente du terrain – contraint de concevoir des piliers de béton comme points d'appui. La disposition intérieure affiche une division spatiale claire et nette entre les zones de jour et de nuit, séparées par l'escalier qui conduit au sous-sol, avec un accès extérieur rendu possible par la déclivité du terrain.

Zu dem Stil von Souto de Moura muss man fast nichts anmerken, denn jeder Liebhaber der Architektur kennt seine Begeisterung für die Genauigkeit und seine extreme Empfindsamkeit für die Umgebung. Dieses Haus in Cascais ist ein weiteres Werk des portugiesischen Architekten. Es wirkt aber aufgrund der verwendeten Materialien und der Annäherung an die architektonische Tradition des Ortes etwas wärmer als seine anderen Gebäude. Das Haus stützt sich auf ein Halbsouterrain, in dem sich die Waschküche und die funktionellen Einrichtungen befinden. Dieses Halbsouterrain dient als Fundament für das Gebäude, das senkrecht zur Neigung des Geländes steht. Deshalb mussten Betonpfeiler als Stützen eingeplant werden. Die innere Aufteilung unterscheidet deutlich zwischen den tagsüber und nachts bewohnten Bereichen, die durch eine Treppe getrennt sind. Das Untergeschoss erreicht man aufgrund der Neigung des Geländes auch direkt von außen.

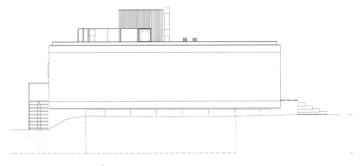

› **Side elevation** Élévation latérale Seitenansicht

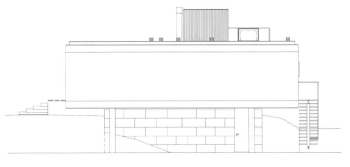

› **Side elevation** Élévation latérale Seitenansicht

White dominates throughout the house, both inside and along the exterior façades.

Le blanc domine toute l'habitation, tant dans les intérieurs que sur les façades.

Die Farbe Weiß herrscht im gesamten Haus vor, sowohl im Inneren als auch an der Fassade.

Residence on the French Riviera

Résidence sur la Côte d'Azur

Residenz an der Côte d'Azur

The French Riviera has long been a vacation area associated with luxury and privilege. This building from the early 20th century was refurbished to endow the rooms with greater continuity and fully open them out to the sea, without making any modification to the original structure on the exterior. Three sharply differentiated spaces were created on the ground floor: a studio, a wonderfully original sitting room and a dining room with a modern design. The basement, which was also subjected to an overhaul, now contains a spectacular gym and spa. The apparent simplicity of the decoration in fact conceals an elegant, audacious and personal style. A terrace, covered by light awnings in some areas, allows the residents to enjoy the outdoor spaces and extraordinary views of the sea at any time of the day, especially during sunset.

De tout temps, la Côte d'Azur est une destination de vacances associée au luxe et aux ambiances chic. Cette construction du début du siècle a été réhabilitée dans le but de fluidifier l'espace et en même temps ouvrir les pièces sur la mer, sans pour autant toucher à l'originalité de la structure extérieure. Le rez-de-chaussée offre trois espaces bien différenciés : un studio, un splendide salon très original et une salle à manger au design contemporain. Le sous-sol, également entièrement remodelé, abrite aujourd'hui une zone de fitness et de spa extraordinaire. L'agencement, d'une sobriété apparente, découvre, en réalité, un style audacieux, élégant et personnel. Une terrasse, recouverte par endroits de légers vélums, permet de profiter des espaces extérieurs et des vues sur la mer à couper le souffle, à toute heure de la journée. Les crépuscules, vus de ce coin de la maison, semblent se prolonger à l'infini.

Die Côte d'Azur war immer schon ein Ferienziel, mit dem man Luxus und eine gepflegte Atmosphäre verband. Dieses zu Beginn des Jahrhunderts entstandene Haus wurde umgebaut, um die Räume durchgängiger zu machen und vollständig zum Meer hin zu öffnen. Dabei wurden allerdings keine Eingriffe an der äußeren Originalstruktur vorgenommen. Im Erdgeschoss entstanden drei deutlich voneinander unterscheidbare Bereiche: ein Arbeitszimmer, ein wundervolles, sehr originelles Wohnzimmer und ein modern gestaltetes Speisezimmer. Im Untergeschoss, das ebenfalls stark verändert wurde, gibt es nun einen besonders schönen Fitnessraum mit Whirlpool. Die scheinbare Einfachheit der Dekoration drückt in Wirklichkeit einen gewagten, eleganten und sehr persönlichen Stil aus. Die Terrasse, die teilweise von leichten Markisen bedeckt ist, wird zum idealen Ort, um den Aufenthalt im Freien und den unglaublich schönen Blick auf das Meer zu jeder Tageszeit genießen zu können.

A terrace covered by light awnings makes it possible to take advantage of the outdoor spaces and fabulous views of the sea at any time of day.

Une terrasse recouverte de légers vélums permet de bénéficier des espaces extérieurs et d'incroyables vues sur la mer à toute heure du jour.

Die Terrasse, die von leichten Markisen bedeckt ist, ist der ideale Ort, um den Aufenthalt im Freien und den unglaublich schönen Blick auf das Meer zu jeder Tageszeit zu genießen.

The basement, which was also subjected to an extensive overhaul, now contains a spectacular gym and spa.

Le sous-sol, soumis également à une profonde réhabilitation, abrite une zone de fitness et de spa spectaculaire.

Im Untergeschoss, das ebenfalls stark verändert wurde, gibt es nun einen besonders schönen Fitnessraum mit Whirlpool.

House in Costa Brava

Maison sur la Costa Brava

Haus an der Costa Brava

This residential complex was constructed in 1965 and houses two homes for two families. Both families decided to update their properties as well as adjust the interior to their new needs. The clients requested the style to be respected and to modify only that which was necessary. The interior modifications are designed to make the interiors habitable and solve constructive architectural problems, which have emerged over the years due to the proximity to the sea. The interior was paved with jatoba wood and the exterior with iroko wood. The new white aluminium frames have adjustable blinds which control the sunlight that enters the house. The walls were covered in plaster and transparent glass was used for the railings, in order not to block the views of the sea.

Cet ensemble résidentiel, construit en 1965, abrite deux habitations pour deux familles qui ont décidé de les rénover tout en adaptant les programmes domestiques à leurs nouveaux besoins. A la demande de leurs clients, les architectes choisis ont respecté le style et n'ont modifié que ce qui était indispensable. Ils ont axé leur projet sur une restauration soignée de l'intérieur pour en favoriser l'habitabilité et la recherche de solutions pour pallier les pathologies de construction surgies au fil des ans et dues à la proximité de la mer. L'intérieur a donc été recouvert de bois exotique de jatova et l'extérieur d'iroko. La nouvelle charpente dotée d'aluminium blanc a des stores réglables qui gèrent l'arrivée de la lumière solaire dans la maison. Les murs ont été revêtus de plâtre et les mains courantes réalisées en verre transparent, pour ne pas faire obstacle à la vue sur la mer.

Dieser Wohnkomplex wurde 1965 errichtet und besteht aus zwei Einfamilienhäusern. Beide Familien beschlossen, ihr Haus zu renovieren und gleichzeitig die Räume an ihre neuen Anforderungen anzupassen. Die Kunden baten die Architekten, den existierenden Stil bei diesem Umbau zu respektieren und nur das Notwendigste zu ändern. Deshalb ging man sehr respektvoll mit den Innenräumen um. Sie sollten bewohnbarer gemacht werden und die Probleme der Struktur gelöst werden, die sich mit der Zeit durch die Meeresnähe ergeben haben. So wurden die Böden im Inneren mit Jatobaholz und außen mit Irokoholz belegt. Die Fenster- und Türrahmen sind aus weißem Aluminium und es wurden einstellbare Jalousien angebracht, mit denen man das Sonnenlicht, das ins Haus fällt, regulieren kann. Die Wände wurden mit Gips verputzt und Geländer aus transparentem Glas geschaffen, so dass der Blick auf das Meer nicht behindert wird.

› Ground floor   Rez-de-chaussée   Erdgeschoss

› First floor   Premier étage   Erstes Obergeschoss

The starkness of the spaces and the finishing of details through simple but sophisticated design are the outstanding features of this refurbishment.

La nudité des espaces et la finition des détails, fruit d'un design sobre et raffiné, sont les aspects qui caractérisent cette oeuvre de restauration intérieure.

Die kahlen Räume und die einfache und raffinierte Dekoration prägen diese Renovierung der Innenräume.

Residence in Tijucopava
Résidence à Tijucopava
Residenz in Tijucopava

This elegant house seems to have been designed to allow its owners to experience its seaside location with particular intensity, as the impressively large windows leave the sitting room and dining room completely exposed to the exterior. Wind and sunlight pass through these windows to penetrate into the rooms, all distinguished by their modern design and pure lines. The use of white emphasizes the interplay of forms and levels that has been established in the interior. Although the house is large, the layout and design of the volumes create a sensation of lightness and luminosity. Outside, a terrace overlooking the sea, a swimming pool and a well-kept garden provide an idyllic setting for relaxing, reading, playing and, above all, enjoying the breathtaking views of the sea.

Cette élégante demeure semble avoir été conçue pour que ses propriétaires profitent intensément de la proximité de la mer. D'impressionnantes baies vitrées ouvrent entièrement le salon et la salle à manger sur le paysage. La brise et la lumière entrent par les fenêtres et inondent les pièces au design moderne et aux lignes claires. Le blanc accentue le jeu de formes et de niveaux généré à l'intérieur. Malgré les dimensions importantes de la demeure, l'agencement et le design des volumes produisent un effet de légèreté et de luminosité. A l'extérieur, une terrasse face à la mer, une piscine et un jardin bien agencé forgent un environnement idyllique pour profiter des moments de repos ou de lecture, de jeux, et, surtout, des spectaculaires vues sur la mer.

Dieses elegante Wohnhaus scheint eigens zu dem Zweck erbaut zu sein, seine Besitzer intensiv die Nähe zum Meer erleben zu lassen. Riesige Fenster lassen die Landschaft fast ohne Unterbrechungen in das Wohnzimmer und das Speisezimmer eindringen. Ebenso gelangen durch diese Fenster reichlich Luft und Licht in die modern gestalteten Räume mit ihren perfekten und reinen Linien. Die Farbe Weiß unterstreicht das Spiel mit den Formen und Ebenen im Inneren. Obwohl das Haus sehr groß ist, wirkt es aufgrund der Anordnung und Gestaltung der einzelnen Gebäudeteile leicht und hell. Eine Terrasse zum Meer, ein Swimmingpool und ein gepflegter Garten umgeben das Haus, eine wundervolle Umgebung zum Entspannen und Lesen, zum Spielen und vor allem zum Genießen des wundervollen Blicks auf den Ozean.

Alongside the swimming pool, a wooden surface and a meticulously landscaped garden provide an ideal place for enjoying the sea breeze.

A côté de la piscine, une surface de bois et une zone paysagée aux lignes parfaites sont le lieu idéal pour profiter de la brise marine.

Am Swimmingpool bilden eine Holzfläche und ein begrünter Bereich mit perfekten Linien den idealen Ort, um die Meeresbrise zu genießen.

The lines of the construction create an interesting interplay of volumes and levels further accentuated by the use of white that emphasizes the forms of the house.

Les lignes de construction créent un intéressant jeu de volumes et de niveaux accentué par le blanc, qui rehausse les formes de la demeure.

Die Linien der Konstruktion lassen ein interessantes Spiel aus Formen und Ebenen entstehen, das von der Farbe Weiß unterstrichen wird.

The breeze and sunshine enter through the large windows and enrich the interiors, which are decorated with exquisite taste.

La brise et la lumière entrent par d'amples baies vitrées et inondent des intérieurs décorés avec un goût exquis.

Luft und Licht dringen durch die großen Fenster ein und durchfluten die Räume, die mit sehr viel Geschmack gestaltet sind.

Villa Positano

The intervention in this fabulous Italian villa, which once formed part of a monastery, was undertaken with the intention of creating a modern space within a historical setting. This reinterpretation of architectural tradition gave rise to a majestic interior, dominated by the great height of the sitting room and the building's original tiles, which date from the 18th and 19th centuries. In order to adapt the tiles to a modern style, a highly distinctive application method was developed. The tiles were applied to a long 2-ft-wide strip that crosses the sitting room and dining room, adjusting to their contours and creating, as it advances, different functional elements in each room: a vertical decorative panel and side table in the sitting room and a table and lighting support in the dining room. In the main bedroom, the bed rests on a platform that is also clad with tiles.

La restauration de cette fantastique résidence italienne, qui, autrefois, faisait partie d'un monastère, vise à créer un espace contemporain au sein d'un contexte historique. L'interprétation des traditions architecturales débouche sur la création d'un intérieur majestueux, dans lequel on remarque l'importante hauteur du salon et la céramique datant des XVIIIe et XIXe siècles. Pour adapter cette céramique à un style contemporain, on a procédé à une méthode d'application très moderne. Un élément tout en longueur, de 60 cm de largeur et paré de ces carreaux de céramique, traverse le salon et la salle à manger, s'adaptant à ses dénivellations et créant, lors de son passage dans chaque pièce, un élément fonctionnel différent : panneau vertical décoratif et table d'appoint au salon, table et colonne d'éclairage dans la salle à manger. Dans la chambre à coucher principal, le lit est posé sur une plateforme également revêtue de céramique.

Bei der Umgestaltung dieses wundervollen Hauses in Italien, das zu einem Kloster gehörte, wollte man eine zeitgenössische Wohnumgebung innerhalb eines historischen Kontextes schaffen. Durch die Neuinterpretation der architektonischen Traditionen entstanden herrschaftliche Räume, unter denen vor allem das Wohnzimmer durch seine Höhe und die Originalkeramik aus dem 18. und 19. Jh. auffällt. Um die Keramiken an den modernen Stil anzupassen, verwendete man sie auf sehr ungewöhnliche Weise. Ein längliches, 60 cm breites Element, das mit diesen Kacheln verkleidet ist, durchquert das Wohnzimmer und das Speisezimmer und folgt den verschiedenen Ebenen, wobei es in jedem Raum zu einem anderen, funktionellen Element wird. Im Salon formt es eine senkrechte, dekorative Platte und einen kleinen Tisch. Im Speisezimmer formt es den Tisch und die Halterung für die Beleuchtung. Das Bett im großen Schlafzimmer steht auf einer Plattform, die ebenfalls gekachelt ist.

The apparent simplicity of the terrace belies the subtlety of the forms, which highlight the natural setting.

La simplicité apparente de la terrasse réside dans la subtilité des formes qui met en valeur l'environnement naturel.

Die Schönheit der Terrasse, die offensichtlich sehr einfach gehalten ist, entsteht durch die subtilen Formen, die die umgebende Natur unterstreichen.

The intervention in this Italian house sought to create a modern space within a historical context.

La restauration de cette fantastique résidence italienne, vise à créer un espace contemporain au sein d'un contexte historique.

Ziel des Eingriffes an diesem Haus in Italien war, moderne Räume innerhalb eines historischen Kontextes zu schaffen.

The reinterpretation of architectural traditions resulted in a majestic interior, decorated in a very distinctive style.

L'interprétation des traditions architecturales débouche sur la création d'un intérieur majestueux, selon une esthétique de décoration très particulière.

Die Interpretation der architektonischen Traditionen hatte diese majestätischen Innenräume zum Ergebnis, die in einem recht eigentümlichen Stil dekoriert sind.

The formula devised for reusing the tiles recovered from the old building was marked by a great respect for these materials.

La formule employée pour réutiliser la céramique récupérée de l'ancienne construction met en valeur ce matériau.

Die Art und Weise, wie die Keramik des Originalgebäudes wieder verwendet wird, führte zu einem sehr respektvollen Umgang mit diesem Material.

Tagomago House

Maison Tagomago

Tagomago Haus

This house is situated by the sea in a typically Mediterranean setting of pines and junipers. The lot slopes gently before reading the edge of a sleep cliff, as if it were a balcony with wide-ranging views stretching toward the horizon. The intense sunlight combines with the green of the trees and the blue of the sea to enhance the austere, meditative forms of the complex. The property's use as a family vacation home led to it being organized around a main nucleus that is surrounded by a series of small pavilions with a degree of autonomy; this set-up allows for flexibility, in accordance with the number of guests at any one time. The construction took advantage of traditional materials typical of the area, such as the stone on the façades and walls, the woodwork and the flooring on the terraces. The small tiled vaults in the concrete roof also follow the traditional model.

Cette résidence, située face à la mer, est plongée dans une flore et faune typiquement méditerranéennes. Le terrain légèrement en pente vient mourir sur une grande falaise, à l'instar d'un immense balcon s'ouvrant sur l'horizon splendide. La lumière intense, le vert de la forêt et le bleu de la mer encadrent ces formes à la fois austères et sereines. Servant de maison familiale de vacances, la demeure s'articule autour d'un axe central et d'une série de pièces ou petits pavillons jouissant d'une certaine autonomie. Cela permet une utilisation assez flexible en fonction du nombre d'habitants. Les matériaux de construction employés sont traditionnels et typiques de la zone, à l'image de la pierre des façades, ou du bois des menuiseries et des sols des terrasses. Les planchers entre deux niveaux sont également réalisés dans le style traditionnel et sont composés de poutres de béton et de travées en céramique.

Dieses Haus steht in einer typischen Mittelmeerlandschaft. Das Grundstück hat eine leichte Neigung, die zu einer hohen Steilküste führt, einer Art Balkon, von dem aus man einen wundervollen Ausblick hat. Das intensive Licht, das Grün des Waldes und das Blau des Meeres umrahmen das Gebäude mit seinen schlichten und ruhigen Formen. Da das Gebäude einer Familie als Ferienwohnung dient, wurde es um ein gemeinsames Zentrum herum in Form von einzelnen Komplexen oder kleinen Pavillons angelegt, die relativ unabhängig voneinander sind. So kann es jeweils der Anzahl von Feriengästen entsprechend benutzt werden. Für den Bau verwendete man traditionelle und typische Materialien aus der Region wie den Naturstein an den Fassaden und das Holz für die Schreinerarbeiten und Terrassenböden. Auch das Fachwerk ist im traditionellen Stil gehalten, es besteht aus Betonträgern und Gewölben aus Keramik.

The low height of this house with a traditional structure does not impinge on the typically Mediterranean paradise of pine and spruce trees that surronds it.

La faible hauteur de cette demeure, de structure traditionnelle, n'altère en rien le paysage typiquement méditerranéen de pins et de sabines où elle se love.

Da das Haus relativ niedrig und im traditionellen Stil gebaut wurde, verändert es nicht die typisch mediterrane Landschaft voller Pinien und Sadebäumen, in der es steht.

The mild climate in this region led the architects to draw up spacious outdoor areas where the pleasant temperatures of the island can be enjoyed all year round.

Le climat doux de cette zone a conduit les architectes à concevoir de spacieuses zones extérieures où l'on jouit toute l'année d'une agréable température insulaire.

Das milde Klima in dieser Region führte dazu, dass die Architekten große Außenbereiche anlegten, in denen man das ganze Jahr über die angenehme Temperatur genießen kann.

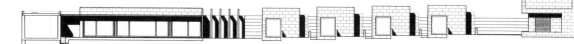

› Front elevation   Élévation frontale   Vorderansicht

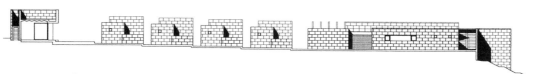

› Rear elevation   Élévation arrière   Hinteransicht

House in Ixtapa

Maison à Ixtapa

Haus in Ixtapa

This house is located on the Guerrero Coast, on the shores of the Pacific Ocean, in a stunning landscape set off by the calm expanse of the sea, only broken by a series of islets. The balance between architecture and nature is evident in the overall design of the house. The structure is made of reinforced concrete and extremely resistant glass panels that enclose a domestic program comprising the kitchen, dining room and terrace which make up the heart of the home. Sliding glass doors open to unite the interior and exterior spaces, while skylights allow additional light to filter into the rooms. White is the dominant color, but it is complemented by dark wood and splashes of color in the accessories, which serve to highlight the sensation of spaciousness and luminosity.

Située au bord de l'océan Pacifique, cette habitation est implantée sur la côte de Guerrero. Le paysage exceptionnel affiche une mer calme parsemée de petits îlots rompant son harmonie. L'équilibre entre architecture et nature caractérise la conception d'ensemble de cet édifice. La structure est faite de béton armé et de panneaux de verre très résistants qui abritent un univers familial où la cuisine, la salle à manger et la terrasse forgent l'âme de la demeure. Des portes de verre coulissantes s'ouvrent pour relier les espaces intérieurs et extérieurs, et les velux diffusent la lumière dans les pièces. Le blanc domine, contrebalancé par les bois sombres et les touches de couleurs des accessoires, pour accroître la sensation d'espace et de luminosité.

Dieses Haus steht am Pazifischen Ozean, an der Küste Guerrero. Es ist von einer wundervollen Landschaft umgeben, deren prägendstes Element der ruhige Ozean ist, in dem kleine Felseninseln die Harmonie der glatten Wasserfläche unterbrechen. Die Planer haben ein perfektes Gleichgewicht zwischen der Architektur und der Natur geschaffen. Die Struktur besteht aus Stahlbeton und sehr widerstandsfähigen Glaspaneelen. In dieser Struktur befindet sich das Herzstück des Hauses, nämlich die Küche, das Speisezimmer und die Terrasse. Gläserne Schiebetüren können geöffnet werden, um die inneren und äußeren Räume miteinander zu vereinen; durch Dachfenster fällt noch zusätzliches Licht ins Innere. Die dominierende Farbe ist Weiß, unterbrochen von dunklem Holz und Farbtupfern in Form von Dekorationselementen. So wird noch mehr Weite und Helligkeit geschaffen.

The balance between architecture and nature is evident in every part of the house.

L'équilibre instauré entre architecture et nature est visible dans tous les recoins de la maison.

Man findet das Gleichgewicht, das zwischen der Architektur und der Natur herrscht, in allen Winkeln des Hauses.

The predominantly pale colors are offset by the darker tone of some furnishings and decorative elements.

La dominance des tons clairs est ponctuée des touches sombres de certaines pièces de mobilier et d'éléments de décoration.

Die dominierenden hellen Farben werden durch dunkle Farbflecken unterbrochen, die durch bestimmte Möbelstücke und Dekorationselemente entstehen.

Winer Residence
Résidence Winer
Residenz Winer

This project grew out of a pre-existing summer home measuring a mere 700 sq. ft. It was decided to add a new volume spread over 1,185 sq. ft, thereby enlarging the original building and adapting it to the needs of a numerous family. This new extension intended to provide more spaces for relaxing and sleeping, as well as endowing the various areas with greater intimacy and preserving the intimate atmosphere of a small home. The design for the new building was similar to that of the earlier one, in terms of both the general architecture and the details. A transparent façade giving on to the beach runs along side the rooms, creating the sensation of a single, continuous space. Resistant materials appropriate to the area's climate were used, along with a number of elements typical of this coastal region.

Le projet part d'une construction préexistante d'à peine 65 m². Afin d'agrandir cette résidence d'été et de l'adapter aux besoins d'une famille plus importante, il a été décidé d'ajouter un nouveau volume de 110 m². Cette nouvelle surface est collée à l'ancienne maison afin d'ajouter de l'espace pour vivre et dormir, accroître l'intimité des diverses zones tout en maintenant l'ambiance accueillante d'une maison de petites dimensions. Le design du nouvel édifice est semblable à celui qui existe déjà, dans l'implantation, l'architecture et les détails. Orientée vers la plage, une façade transparente parcourt toutes les pièces et génère une sensation d'espace unique et fluide. Les matériaux de construction employés sont résistants, en fonction des conditions climatiques de la zone, et sont agrémentés d'une gamme d'éléments typiques de la côte.

Ein bereits existierendes, nur 65 m² großes Gebäude war Gegenstand dieses Um- und Ausbaus. Um das Sommerhaus zu vergrößern und an die Anforderungen einer größeren Familie anzupassen, beschloss man, einen 110 m² großen Anbau zu konstruieren. Dieses neue Gebäude wurde mit dem alten Haus verbunden, um Raum zu schaffen, eine intimere Atmosphäre in den verschiedenen Bereichen entstehen zu lassen und gleichzeitig die gemütliche Atmosphäre des kleinen Hauses zu bewahren. Die Gestaltung des neuen Gebäudes ähnelt in architektonischen sowie dekorativen Details der des bereits existierenden Hauses. Das Haus ist zum Meer ausgerichtet und seine transparente Fassade, die sich an allen Zimmern entlang erstreckt, lässt den Raum einheitlich wirken. Es wurden widerstandsfähige Baumaterialien verwendet, die den klimatischen Bedingungen gerecht werden, sowie eine Reihe typischer Baustoffe dieser Region.

The resistant materials used in this building are suited to the harsh weather conditions and arid nature of the area.

Les matériaux résistants employés sur cette construction se conjuguent à l'aridité de l'environnement, soumis aux dures conditions climatiques de la zone.

Die widerstandsfähigen Materialien, die für dieses Gebäude benutzt wurden, passen zum rauen Klima un der Trockenheit in dieser Region.

The façade that gives on to the beach is entirely fronted with glass, creating the sensation of a single, continuous space.

La façade qui donne sur la plage est tout en verre, ce qui génère une sensation d'espace unique et fluide.

Die Fassade zum Strand hin ist vollständig verglast, so dass der Eindruck eines einzigen und durchgehenden Raums entsteht.

House in Guaecá

Maison à Guaecá

Haus in Guaecá

This house stands on a lot next to the Guaecá beach. Two distinct settings vie for its attention: the ocean on one side and the lush mountains on the other. The building, with a basement, ground floor and upper level, presents two very distinct faces: on one side, the south and east façades, surrounded by terraces at each level and refreshed by the water of the swimming pool, open out on to the sea through the use of light, transparent materials like laminated wood, aluminum and glass; in contrast, the north and west are closed in the face of the large mountainous mass and are dominated by reinforced concrete, with barely a small balcony to interrupt the otherwise unbroken surface. Both the exterior structure and the interior layout emphasize the two-pronged approach to the house, along with its impeccable adaptation to its surroundings.

Sur un terrain jouxtant la plage de Guaecá, s'élève une construction convoitée par deux prétendants : la mer et les montagnes luxuriantes. L'édifice, avec sous-sol, rez-de-chaussée et premier étage, offre deux visages bien distincts. D'un côté, les façades sud et est, entourées à chaque étage de terrasses et rafraîchies par les eaux de la piscine, s'ouvrent vers la mer par le biais de matériaux légers et transparents, à l'instar du bois laminé, de l'aluminium et du verre. De l'autre côté, au nord et à l'ouest, elles se ferment devant un grand massif montagneux. Ces façades sont faites de béton armé dont un petit balcon interrompt l'aspect hermétique. Structure et distribution renforcent la double orientation de la demeure, qui se fond ainsi parfaitement à l'environnement.

Auf einem Grundstück am Strand Guaecá erhebt sich dieses Gebäude, dessen Umgebung von zwei landschaftlichen Elementen geprägt ist: dem Meer und den üppig bewachsenen Bergen. Das Gebäude verfügt über ein Kellergeschoss, ein Erdgeschoss und eine erste Etage und ist von außen durch zwei sehr unterschiedliche Fassaden gekennzeichnet. Die Süd- und Ostfassade, die auf jeder Etage von Terrassen und Swimmingpools umgeben sind, wurden aus leichten und transparenten Materialien wie Lagenholz, Aluminium und Glas konstruiert, so dass sie sich zum Meer hin öffnen. Auf der Nord- und Westseite, ist das Haus zu dem großen, gegenüberliegenden Berg hin geschlossen. Diese Fassaden bestehen aus Stahlbeton und einem kleinen Balkon, der diese Geschlossenheit unterbricht. Sowohl die Struktur als auch die Verteilung verstärken diesen doppelten Charakter des Hauses sowie die perfekte Anpassung an die Umgebung.

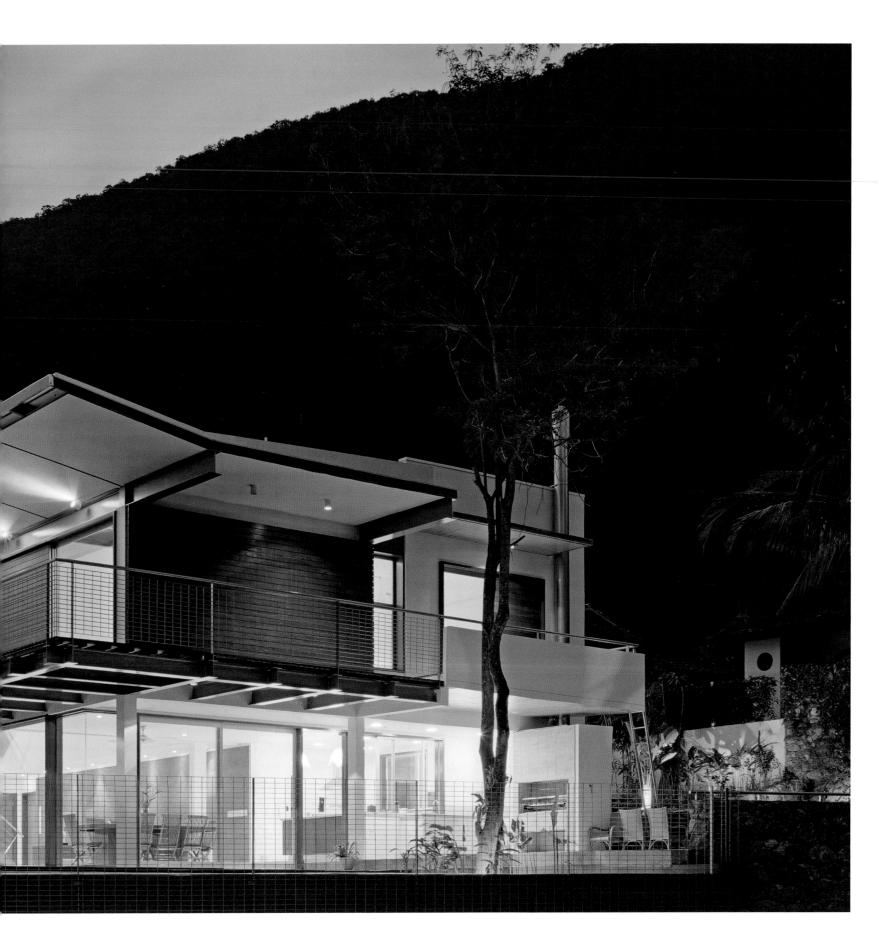

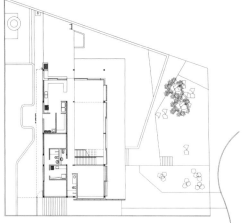

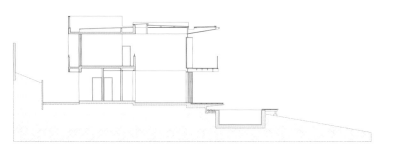

› Location plan Plan de situation Umgebungsplan

› Longitudinal section Section longitudinale Längsschnitt

Both the structure and the layout reinforce the dual orientation of the home and its perfect adaptation to its surroundings.

Tant la structure que la distribution renforcent la double orientation de la demeure et sa parfaite intégration à l'environnement.

Sowohl die Struktur als auch die Aufteilung verstärken diesen doppelten Charakter des Hauses und die perfekte Anpassung an die Umgebung.

243

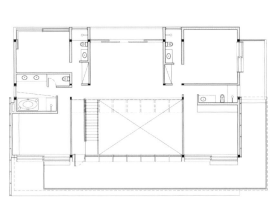

› Ground floor Rez-de-chaussée Erdgeschoss

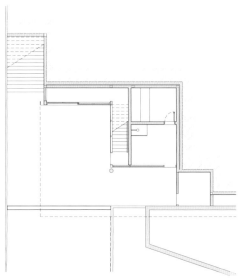

› First floor Premier étage Erstes Obergeschoss

Roozen House
Maison Roozen
Roozen Haus

This house, built on a hill on the River Margaret dunes in Western Australia, lies 440 yards from the sea, facing southwest. The building's architectural expression is an abstract interpretation of the magic of this setting, manifested by a series of devices designed to create optical illusions. There are three elements that enhance and accompany specific views of the landscapes and sea. One is the main axis of the triangular site, which faces the sea; the second is the outline of the Leeuwin Ridge Cape, toward the southeast, which forms another expanse of water, and the third is a small Greek church to the northeast. These elements are framed by various parts of the building's structure, which is rooted in the land and projects outward toward the wild and beautiful landscape.

Cette maison, construite sur une colline, dans les dunes du fleuve Margaret à l'ouest de l'Australie, est orientée vers le sud ouest, à 400 m de la mer. L'expression architecturale de l'édifice est une interprétation abstraite de la magie du lieu qui se reflète sur le plan de la construction par le biais d'une série de dispositifs créant des illusions d'optique. Trois éléments exaltent et accompagnent certaines vues panoramiques terrestres et maritimes. Le premier est l'axe principal de cet emplacement triangulaire, orienté vers la mer, le deuxième est la ligne du cap Leeuwin Ridge vers le sud-est, qui forme une autre mer, et le troisième, une petite icône culturelle : une église grecque sur la partie nord-ouest. Ces éléments sont encadrés en divers points par la structure qui, ancrée sur le sol, se projette vers l'extérieur dans ce paysage à la beauté sauvage.

Dieses Haus, auf einer Anhöhe in den Dünen des Flusses Margaret im Westen von Australien, öffnet sich in Richtung Südwesten und ist nur 400 m vom Meer entfernt. Die Architektur des Gebäudes ist eine abstrakte Interpretation der Magie des Standortes, bestehend aus einer Reihe von baulichen Elementen, die optische Illusionen erzeugen. Drei Elemente untermalen und begleiten besondere Ausblicke auf das Land und das Meer. Eines davon ist die Hauptachse dieses dreieckigen Standortes, der zum Meer hin ausgerichtet ist. Das zweite sind die Umrisse des Kap Leeuwin Ridge im Südosten, die ein anderes Meer entstehen lassen; und das dritte Element ist eine kleine Kulturikone, eine griechische Kirche im Nordwesten. Für diese Elemente wurde an verschiedenen Stellen ein Rahmen in der Struktur des Hauses geschaffen, die in der Erde verankert ist, sich aber zu der wilden und wunderbaren Landschaft hin öffnet.

The architectural expression of the building is an abstract interpretation of the magic of the location.

L'expression architecturale de l'édifice est une interprétation abstraite de la magie du lieu.

Der architektonische Ausdruck des Gebäudes ist eine abstrakte Interpretation der Magie des Ortes.

› Longitudinal section Section longitudinale Längsschnitt

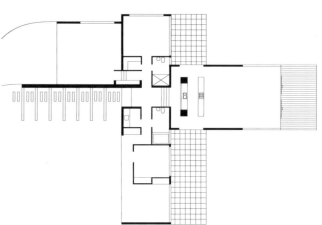

› Plan Plan Grundriss

M House
Maison M
Haus M

This project's composition posed a challenge: to resolve and value the dual conditions of the site. As a house in the desert, the building had to create an intimate space amidst the vast landscape. On the other hand, the presence of the ocean called for the house to open up towards the horizon. The architectural plans started with this contradiction: to establish a dialectical relationship between closure and opening, opacity and transparency. Following local building traditions, the architects first established a site and then demarcated the land with walls that preserve the intimacy of the exterior zones, while relating them to the interior space of the house. The house is divided into three stepped levels that create relationships among one another and permit the residents to perceive the ocean from even the most remote spots.

Le principal défi dans la composition du projet consiste en résoudre la dualité des conditions de l'emplacement choisi pour implanter la construction. D'un côté, une maison dans le désert doit être un espace intime dans l'immensité du territoire et de l'autre, la présence de la mer invite à s'ouvrir sur l'horizon. Le plan part de cette contradiction pour instaurer une dialectique entre confinement et ouverture, opacité et transparence. Le modèle des constructions environnantes présente une enceinte, une délimitation du terrain par des murs pour préserver l'intimité des zones extérieures en relation avec l'espace intérieur de l'habitation. La maison est divisée en trois volumes qui, au-delà de l'entrée, établissent des liens entre eux, créant une dénivellation de terrain qui laisse apercevoir la mer depuis les espaces plus éloignés de la maison.

Die größte Herausforderung bei der Planung dieses Hauses war die Dualität der Bedingungen an dem Ort, an dem gebaut werden sollte. Einerseits musste das Haus in der Wüste ein intimer Ort inmitten dieser weiten Landschaft sein. Andererseits liegt das Haus am Meer, zu dem es sich öffnen sollte. Bei der Planung ging man genau von diesem Widerspruch aus, um eine dialektische Beziehung zwischen geschlossen und offen, undurchsichtig und durchsichtig zu schaffen. Man folgte dem Beispiel anderer Bauten der Umgebung und schuf ein geschlossenes Gelände, das von Mauern begrenzt wird, die die Privatsphäre der Außenbereiche schützen und eine Beziehung zu den Innenräumen des Hauses schaffen. Das Haus unterteilt sich in drei Blöcke, die, nachdem man es betreten hat, in Beziehung zueinander treten und verschiedene Ebenen schaffen, so dass man das Meer von fast allen Winkeln des Hauses aus sehen kann.

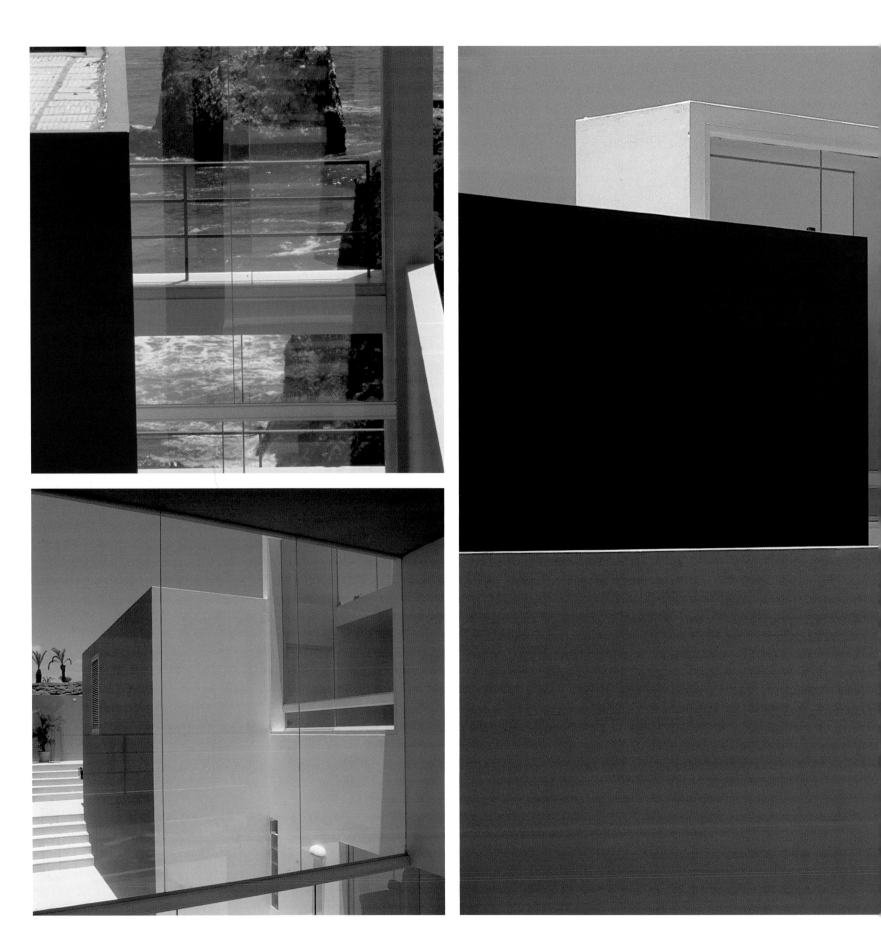

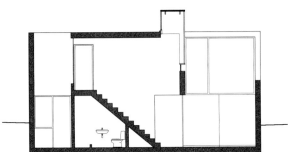

› Longitudinal section Section longitudinale Längsschnitt

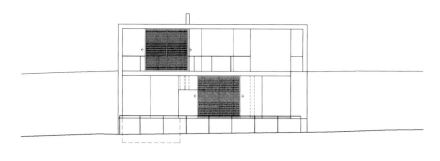

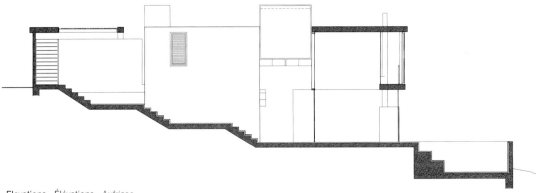

› Elevations Élévations Aufrisse

B House
Maison B
Haus B

The challenge of this construction, situated in one of the most arid deserts in the world, consisted of achieving a totally permeable architecture in which the walls serve the dual function of highlighting the landscape while providing the necessary privacy. Architectural abstraction links the building to the constructional and artistic expressions of the Pre-Columbian era and the Spanish colonial style. Another challenge was posed by the sleeply sloping terrain, which enabled only one façade to face the exterior. Furthermore, the clients wished for separate areas for parents and children, leading to a generational divide on a vertical plane, with the parents occupying the upper floor and the children the lower level, separated by an entresol devoted to the communal service areas.

Outre le fait que cette construction se trouve dans un des déserts les plus arides du monde, le défi à relever était de réaliser une architecture entièrement transparente avec des murs ayant la double fonction d'exalter le paysage tout en préservant l'intimité nécessaire. L'abstraction architecturale relie l'oeuvre aux expressions constructives et artistiques de deux périodes, précolombienne et coloniale espagnole présentes dans la région. Le fait de s'implanter sur un coteau si escarpé ne permettait de réaliser qu'une ouverture en façade pour tourner l'édifice vers l'extérieur. En outre, le souhait des clients de créer des espaces indépendants entre les parents et les enfants a été réalisé en concevant une séparation à la verticale entre les générations : les parents occupent le niveau supérieur et les enfants l'étage inférieur, tous les deux séparés par un entresol destiné aux services communs.

Bei diesem Haus, das sich in einer der trockensten Wüsten der Welt befindet, stellten sich die Planer der Herausforderung, eine absolut durchlässige architektonische Struktur zu schaffen, in der die Wände eine doppelte Funktion erfüllen, nämlich die Landschaft miteinzubeziehen und zugleich für die notwendige Privatsphäre der Bewohner zu sorgen. Die abstrakte Architektur verbindet das Bauwerk mit Elementen der präkolumbianischen Periode und der Zeit der spanischen Kolonisation, die beide in dieser Region präsent sind. Da das Haus auf einem steilen Abhang errichtet wurde, gab es nur eine Seite, die sich nach außen öffnen konnte. Um die Räume der Eltern von denen der Kinder trennen, wurde eine vertikale, Teilung geschaffen, so dass die Eltern im Obergeschoss und die Kinder im Untergeschoss wohnen. Dazwischen befindet sich ein Zwischengeschoss mit allen gemeinschaftlich genutzten Räumen.

The strong colors applied to this building's walls emphasize its forms, in the midst of the arid desert that surrounds it.

Les tonalités extrêmes appliquées sur les murs de cette construction exaltent ses volumes au coeur de l'aridité du désert qui l'accueille.

Die kräftigen Farben der Wände dieses Hauses unterstreichen seine Formen inmitten dieser trockenen Wüstenlandschaft, in der es sich befindet.

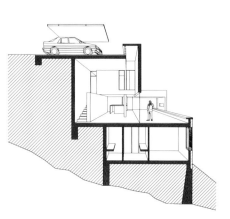

› Perspective Perspective Perspektivzeichnung

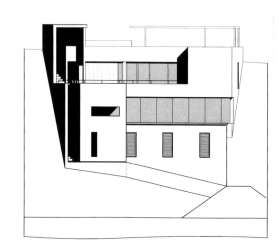

› Elevation Élévation Aufriss

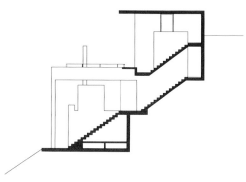

› Section Section Schnitt

Baja House

Maison Baja

Haus Baja

This project took as its starting point the terrain of the lot, which measured 80 ft by 380 ft and offered magnificent panoramic views of the sea on its narrowest sides. In contrast, on lengthways the land is bounded by walls dividing it from the neighboring lots. The location, on a flat platform 26 ft above the level of the Pacific, creates a natural balcony overlooking the sea. The design incorporates techniques and building materials derived from regional traditions that establish connections with vernacular architecture while using a totally modern language. The composition consists of two volumes that break up the elongated proportions of the lot to create a central area between the two, thus reinterpreting the typical Mexican patio. These volumes are finished with thin, pale yellow mortar, which blends into the color scheme of the surrounding desert landscape.

Les conditions du terrain, une parcelle de 25 x 115 m, ont défini le projet. Ses côtés les plus étroits bénéficient de vues panoramiques splendides sur la mer. En contraste, la parcelle est limitée par des terrains voisins mitoyens sur ses flancs les plus longs. L'élévation du terrain, sur un plateau à 8 m au-dessus du niveau de la mer, crée un balcon naturel au-dessus de l'océan Pacifique. La conception intègre des éléments de construction, techniques et matériaux régionaux traditionnels, qui s'unissent à l'architecture vernaculaire grâce à un langage totalement contemporain. La composition s'organise autour de deux volumes qui brisent la longueur du terrain et créent un espace central, entre les deux, qui réinterprète la typologie du patio mexicain. Ces volumes sont réalisés avec du mortier fin dans les tons de jaune clair qui se fond à la palette de couleurs du paysage désertique environnant.

Der Ausgangspunkt bei der Planung dieses Hauses war das 25 x 115 m große Grundstück. Von den schmalen Seiten aus hat man einen wundervollen Blick auf den Ozean. An den Längsseiten wird die Parzelle jedoch durch Mauern von den Nachbargebäuden getrennt. Durch die erhöhte Lage des Grundstücks, auf einer Ebene 8 m über dem Meeresspiegel, entsteht ein natürlicher Balkon über dem Pazifischen Ozean. Für die Gestaltung verwendete man traditionelle Techniken und Baustoffe der Region, die es in einer absolut modernen Sprache mit der einheimischen Architektur verbinden. Das Gebäude besteht aus zwei Formen, die das Grundstück längs unterbrechen und einen zentralen Raum zwischen beiden Gebäudeteilen bilden eine Art Neuinterpretation des typisch mexikanischen Innenhofes. Die Gebäude sind mit feinem Mörtel in hellem Gelb verputzt, das sich ausgezeichnet in das Farbenspiel der umgebenden Wüstenlandschaft einfügt.

The walls are finished with thin mortar painted pale yellow a color that blends into the Mexican desert landscape.

La finition des murs est en mortier fin peint en jaune clair, une tonalité qui s'intègre dans le paysage désertique mexicain.

Die Mauern sind mit feinem Mörtel verputzt und hellgelb gestrichen. Diese Farbe fügt sich perfekt in die mexikanische Wüstenlandschaft ein.

A path zigzags from the terrace on the ground floor, rises up the slope and leads to the beach.

De la terrasse du rez-de-chaussée part un chemin qui zigzague pour pallier la pente et conduire à la plage.

Von der Terrasse im Erdgeschoss führt ein Weg im Zickzack den Abhang entlang bis zum Strand.

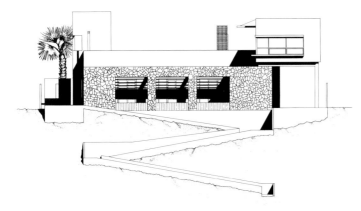

› Elevation Élévation Aufriss

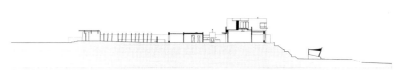

› Cross section Section transversale Querschnitt

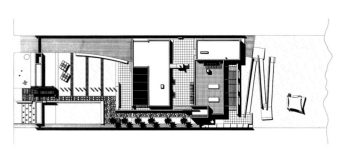

› Ground floor   Rez-de-chaussée   Erdgeschoss

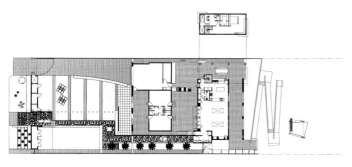

› Plan   Plan   Grundriss

House in Mermaid Beach

Maison à Mermaid Beach

Haus in Mermaid Beach

This project on the Gold Coast in Queensland involved the thorough refurbishment of a home made up of two independent structures. One of the briefs was the establishment of a physical link between the two volumes. Both new and recycled beams were used to join the rear section to the front building. This new area forms a central patio with a roof, fireplace and pool, affording the house's occupants protection from all climatic extremes, as well as providing a close relationship with the sea. The façade overlooking the sea is decorated with a sculptural composition, based on large columns of recycled wood, and this sets the house apart from the other properties nearby.

Ce projet sur la Côte Dorée de Queensland implique la restauration totale d'un édifice déjà existant, composé de structures indépendantes. Une des lignes directrices est d'établir un lien physique entre les deux volumes. Des poutres neuves et recyclées ont été choisies pour relier les sections frontale et dorsale du complexe. Cette zone de liaison façonne un patio central coiffé d'une toiture intérieure, d'une cheminée et d'un bassin, permettant à ses habitants de se protéger des conditions climatiques extrêmes. Le nouveau patio conserve un lien étroit avec la mer. La façade orientée vers la mer est ornée d'une imposante sculpture faite de colonnes de bois recyclé qui la démarque des propriétés voisines.

Für dieses Haus an der Gold Coast in Queensland wurden zwei bereits existierende, unabhängige Gebäude miteinander verbunden und vollständig renoviert. Bei diesem Umbau war eines der wichtigsten Ziele, eine physische Verbindung zwischen den beiden Gebäuden zu schaffen. Dazu wurden neue und alte Träger und Balken verwendet. Das verbindende Element ist ein zentraler, überdachter Innenhof mit einem Kamin und einem Wasserbecken, in den sich die Bewohner bei schlechtem Wetter zurückziehen können. Der neue Hof hat eine sehr enge Beziehung zum Meer. Die zum Meer zeigende Fassade wird durch eine skulpturelle Komposition verziert, die aus großen Säulen aus wieder verwertbarem Holz besteht. Durch diese Fassade hebt sich das Gebäude stark von den umliegenden Häusern ab.

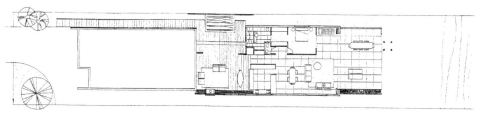

› Plan Plan Grundriss

Capistrano Beach House

Maison à Capistrano Beach

Haus am Capistrano Beach

This house on Capistrano Beach is full of contrasts, in both the interior and exterior. The entrance on the east side is through two iron gates which lead to an intimate, formal vegetable garden enclosed by 6 feet-high glass walls. A concrete "pier" crosses the sand to the porch and front door which face the cliffs and look on to the courtyard garden. The hall follows the curved glass wall and opens dramatically into the spacious living room, with its exposed roof beams and expansive view of the ocean. Along the beach side of the house is a small sitting room shaded by lattice work and a low-ceilinged dining room, both providing more private areas from the living room which through its mahogany and glass doors forms almost part of the beach. The exposed concrete provides attractive sculptural and geometric shapes both inside and outside.

Ce qui définit le mieux cette résidence au bord de la plage, c'est le jeu de contrastes, à l'intérieur comme à l'extérieur. Derrière une façade aux formes droites et angulaires, s'ouvre un monde dominé par la sinuosité des formes arrondies de la structure ainsi que du mobilier qui la décore. Un patio intérieur protégé par des murs incurvés tout en verre accueille un petit jardin soigné. La salle à manger, dominée par les tons clairs, s'ouvre sur ce jardin grâce à trois grandes portes pivotantes de 1,80 m de haut. Aussi bien la petite salle de séjour, protégée par un store, que la salle à manger, basse de plafond, affichent des espaces plus accueillants que le salon, qui, fort de ses trois hauteurs, est la pièce la plus volumineuse de la maison. De la façade qui donne sur la plage surgit une plate-forme de béton ancrée dans le sable, façonnant un vaste porche abrité sous un vélum dépliable qui le protége du rayonnement solaire directe.

Was dieses Strandhaus auszeichnet, ist das Spiel mit den Kontrasten, sowohl innen als auch außen. Hinter einer Fassade mit geraden und eckigen Formen öffnet sich eine Welt, die von den kurvigen und abgerundeten Formen der Struktur und der Möbel dominiert wird. Ein von verglasten und gebogenen Mauern umgebener Innenhof enthält einen kleinen, gepflegten Garten. Das Speisezimmer, in dem helle Farben dominieren, ist durch große, 1,80 m hohe Schwingtüren mit diesem Garten verbunden. Neben dem Speisezimmer befindet sich ein Aufenthaltsraum, der von einer Jalousie geschützt wird und eine niedrige Decke hat. Diese Räume wirken gemütlicher als das Wohnzimmer, das mit seinen drei verschiedenen Höhen der größte Raum des Hauses ist. Die Fassade, die zum Strand hin liegt, entspringt einer im Sand verankerten Betonplattform, die eine große Veranda bildet, über der sich eine Markise spannt, die vor direktem Sonnenlicht schützt.

This building forms part of a chain of family houses built in Capistrano Beach, on the edge of the seashore, right on the sand.

Cette construction s'insère dans une file de demeures individuelles construites dans la localité de Capistrano Beach, au pied de la plage, à même le sable.

Dieses Haus steht in einer Reihe von Einfamilienhäusern, die direkt am Strand auf dem Sand in Capistrano Beach errichtet wurden.

Sunlight pours into the interior on every plane, thanks to the numerous possibilities offered by the use of glass.

La lumière naturelle pénètre à l'intérieur par tous les plans du volume grâce aux nombreuses possibilités qu'offre le verre.

Dank der zahlreichen Glaselemente kann auf allen Ebenen des Baus viel Tageslicht eindringen.

The interior provides variety in the rooms; the sitting room is of double height, the dining room has a low ceiling and the lounge is bathed in light entering from the sides.

L'intérieur affiche des espaces très variés : le salon à double hauteur, la salle à manger à la toiture basse, la salle de séjour baignée de lumière latérale.

Die Räume sind unterschiedlich konzepiert: Das Wohnzimmer mit doppelter Höhe, das Speisezimmer mit niedriger Decke und der Aufenthaltsraum, der Licht von den Seiten erhält.

Residence in Barra do Sahy

Résidence à Barra do Sahy

Residenz in Barra do Sahy

Barra do Sahy is a beach on the northern coast of the Brazilian state of São Paulo. The characteristics of the area's tropical climate—humidity and high temperatures—largely determined the approach to this house, along with two basic considerations: a tight schedule and a limited budget. The construction was conceived as a functional building with simple forms, crowned by a roof that juts out boldly from the mass of the house to protect it from the sun and rain. The interior layout is arranged around seven structural, transversal axes that divide the space regularly into six modules lined up in a row: three for the bedrooms and bathrooms and three for the living room, service area and kitchen. The openings to the southwest and northeast in the bedrooms and kitchen allow air to pass through while also endowing the building with transparency.

Barra do Sahy est une plage de la côte nord de l'état brésilien de São Paulo. Les caractéristiques propres au climat tropical de la zone – humidité et températures élevées – ont en grande partie déterminé la conception de cette demeure, au demeurant soumise à deux impératifs : les restrictions de temps et de budget. La construction est un édifice fonctionnel aux formes simples, surmonté d'une toiture dépassant largement la structure du volume pour la protéger du soleil et de la pluie. La distribution intérieure suit un schéma normal, orchestrée selon sept axes transversaux, divisant l'espace en six modules alignés : trois pour les chambres et les salles de bain, les trois autres accueillant la zone de service et la cuisine. Les ouvertures au sud-ouest et au nord-est des chambres et de la cuisine permettent une ventilation croisée, tout en inscrivant l'édifice sous le signe de la transparence.

Barra do Sahy ist ein Strand an der Nordküste des brasilianischen Staates São Paulo. Das feuchte, tropische Klima der Region mit hohen Temperaturen war ausschlaggebend für die Planung dieses Wohnhauses, die von zwei grundlegenden Faktoren bestimmt wurde: der knappen Zeit, die zur Verfügung stand, und dem beschränkten Budget. Das Haus wurde als ein funktionelles Gebäude mit einfachen Formen angelegt, dessen Dach ziemlich weit über die Mauern übersteht, um das Gebäude vor Sonne und Regen zu schützen. Die innere Struktur bestcht aus einem Rechteck mit sieben Querachsen, die den Raum in sechs aneinander gereihte Module teilen: drei für die Schlafzimmer und Bäder sowie drei für das Wohnzimmer, den Waschraum und die Küche. Die Fenster nach Südwest und Nordost in den Schlafzimmern und der Küche ermöglichen eine gute Belüftung und lassen das Gebäude gleichzeitig sehr transparent wirken.

The bold color scheme sets the tone for the interior decoration of this house.

Une palette chromatique de couleurs audacieuses donne le ton dans la décoration intérieure de cette demeure.

Eine gewagte Farbpalette dominiert die Inneneinrichtung des Hauses.

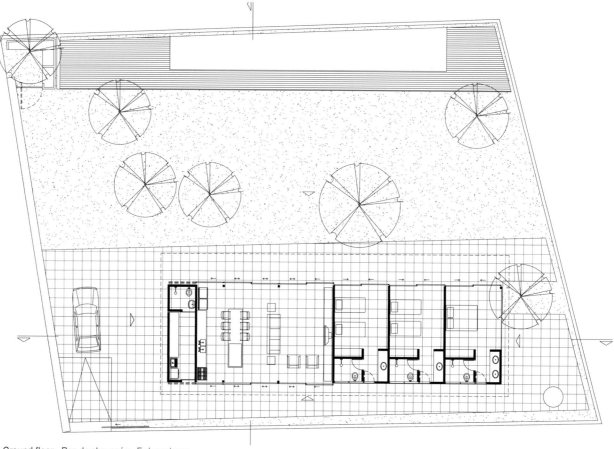

› Ground floor   Rez-de-chaussée   Erdgeschoss

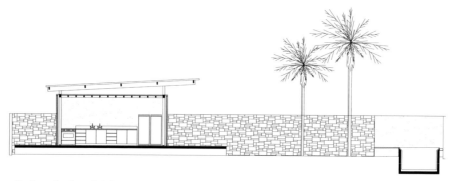

› Section   Section   Schnitt

A sliding glass door allows the bedroom to open on to the terrace, which is connected to a sand garden.

Grâce à des portes vitrées, coulissantes, la chambre à coucher s'ouvre sur la terrasse, qui, à son tour communique avec un jardin de sable.

Das Schlafzimmer besitzt Schiebetüren aus Glas, durch die man es zur Terrasse hin öffnen kann. Sie ist mit einem Sandgarten verbunden.

Scobie House

Maison Scobie

Haus Scobie

Avoca is a small coastal area in the north of Sydney, surrounded by a chain of hills on the end of which this house is situated. It is located in the middle of a natural reserve and enjoys views over the Pacific Ocean. The body of the house is divided into three different layers: the first accommodates the children's, grandparents' and guest bedrooms; the second, the hallway and the living room; and the third, the bedrooms and studies. One important design feature is a wall, aligned north-south, which separates the public space from private. The wall also contains the house's point of entry, a purposeful device that reveals the view to the visitor only after arriving. In the interior, the wall gives order to the building and defines the different areas. At the extreme edges of the house, the structure seems to emerge from the surrounding vegetation.

Avoca est une petite zone côtière du nord de Sydney, entourée d'une chaîne montagneuse à l'extrémité de laquelle se trouve cette résidence, au coeur d'une réserve naturelle, donnant sur l'océan Pacifique. Le corps de l'habitation est divisé en trois niveaux différents : le premier accueille les chambres à coucher des enfants et des grands-parents, ainsi que la chambre d'amis, le deuxième, le vestibule et le salon, et le troisième, la chambre des propriétaires et le studio. Le principal élément de ce projet, un mur aligné sur l'axe nord-sud, sépare l'espace public du privé, et orchestre la distribution de l'espace. Comme c'est le point d'ancrage de l'entrée de la maison, le visiteur ne voit l'intérieur de l'habitation qu'une fois dedans. Aux extrémités extérieures de la maison, la structure semble émerger de la végétation qui l'entoure.

Avoca ist eine kleine, von einer Bergkette umgebene Küstenregion im Norden von Sydney. Oben auf einem dieser Berge befindet sich dieses Haus. Mitten in einem Naturschutzgebiet und mit Ausblick auf den Pazifischen Ozean. Der Körper des Hauses unterteilt sich in drei verschiedene Ebenen: Auf der ersten dieser Ebenen liegen die Schlafzimmer der Kinder und der Großeltern sowie das Gästezimmer, auf der zweiten die Diele und das Wohnzimmer und auf der dritten, das Hauptschlafzimmer und das Arbeitszimmer. Das wichtigste Element dieses Gebäudes ist eine Wand, die eine Nord-Süd-Achse bildet und die gemeinsam bewohnten Räume von den privateren Bereichen trennt. Da sich die Wand auch im Eingangsbereich befindet, erschließt sich das Innere des Hauses nur demjenigen, der es betritt. An den Enden des Hauses scheint die Struktur der umgebenden Vegetation zu entsteigen.

Wood, concrete and steel are combined in this house that emerges from the thick vegetation of a nature reserve.

Bois, béton et acier s'unissent dans cette résidence qui émerge de la dense végétation d'une réserve naturelle.

Holz, Beton und Stahl werden in diesem Haus kombiniert, das inmitten der dichten Vegetation eines Naturparks liegt.

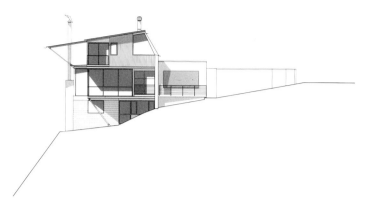

› Elevation Élévation Aufriss

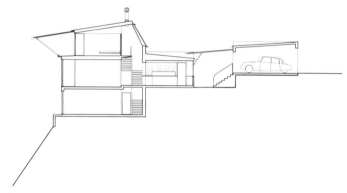

› Cross section Section transversale Querschnitt

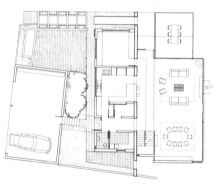

› Ground floor Rez-de-chaussée Erdgeschoss

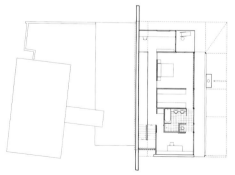

› First floor Premier étage Erstes Obergeschoss

House in LaHave

Maison à LaHave

Haus in LaHave

Two cube-shape buildings float on the hills at the point where the Rive LaHave meets the sea. These two structures—one a home and the other an annex for guests—are aligned on a north-south axis and both face the river and the sea. The wetland between the two hillocks was laid out as a central garden. The two identical structures are set 500 feet apart and are linked visually by concrete walls stretching toward the garden. The entrance is situated to the left of the wall in both buildings; sliding glass doors almost 8 ft in height form the base, while glass panels around the upper floor provide an additional source of natural light. A concrete block contains a fireplace (the starting point for a module incorporating the kitchen and staircase), as well as a fountain that sends water from the roof into the garden.

Deux édifices de forme cubique flottent sur les collines situées dans un lieu où le fleuve LaHave se jette dans la mer. Ces deux structures, résidence et maison d'invités, alignées sur un axe nord-est, sont toutes les deux situées face à la mer. La terre humide entre les deux monticules, forme un jardin central. Les deux volumes identiques, distants de 140 m, sont reliés sur le plan optique par des murs de béton qui se prolongent vers le jardin. Dans les deux édifices, l'entrée est située à gauche du mur. L'espace restant est doté de portes de verres coulissantes de près de 2,5 m de haut, formant le socle où repose l'étage supérieur inondé de lumière naturelle grâce aux panneaux de verre qui l'entourent. Un bloc de béton héberge la cheminée, créant un module qui abrite la cuisine, l'escalier et une fontaine qui déverse son eau de la toiture vers le jardin.

Zwei würfelförmige Gebäude schweben über den Anhöhen des Flusses LaHave, der an dieser Stelle ins Meer fließt. Diese beiden Strukturen, ein Wohnhaus und ein Gästehaus, liegen dem Fluss und dem Meer gegenüber auf einer Nord-Süd-Achse. Auf dem feuchten Land, das zwischen den beiden Hügeln liegt, wurde ein zentraler Garten angelegt. Die beiden identischen Formen stehen 140 m weit voneinander entfernt und werden durch Betonmauern, die sich bis zum Garten erstrecken, visuell vereint. In beiden Gebäuden liegt der Eingang links von der Mauer. Im übrigen Raum bilden fast 2,5 m lange, gläserne Schiebetüren die Basis. Im Obergeschoss fällt das Tageslicht durch die Glasplatten ein, die es umgeben. Ein Betonblock. Ein Betonblock enthält einen Kamin und einen Brunnen aus dem Wasser vom Dach in den Garten sprudelt. Dieses Modul beinhaltet die Küche und das Treppenhaus.

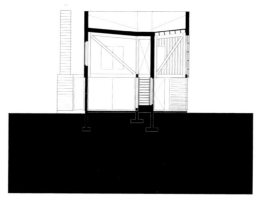

› Elevation Élévation Aufriss

Half of the façade on the ground floor is covered with glass, creating a striking effect of transparency that contrasts with the upper level.

La moitié de la superficie de façade du rez-de-chaussée est tout en verre, produisant ainsi un effet important de transparence qui contraste avec le niveau supérieur.

Die Hälfte der Fassadenfläche des Erdgeschosses ist verglast, so dass diese Ebene im Gegensatz zu dem Obergeschoss sehr transparent wirkt.

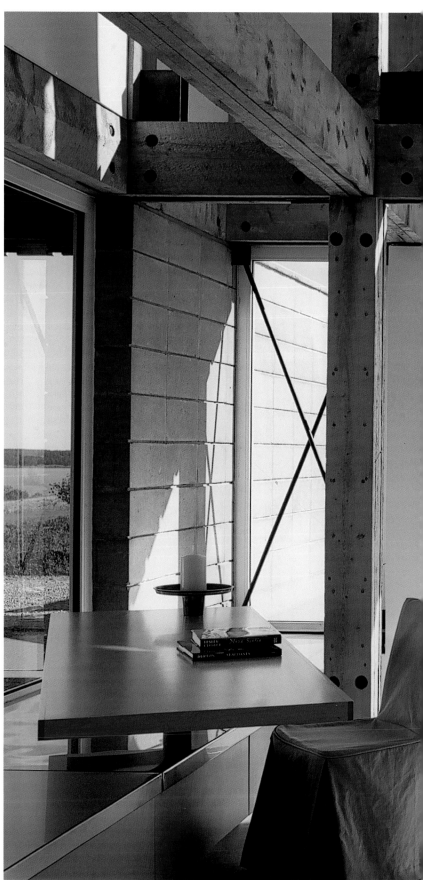

There is a spectacular contrast between the warmth of the wood on the vertical lines and the coldness of the plaster and concrete cladding the horizontal planes.

Le contraste est particulièrement spectaculaire entre la chaleur du bois qui domine à la verticale et la froideur du gypse et du béton des plans horizontaux.

Der Kontrast zwischen der Wärme des Holzes an den Wänden und der Kälte des Gipses und Betons an Böden und Decken ist überwältigend.

Cutler Residence
Résidence Cutler
Residenz Cutler

This remote lot, tucked into a cornice facing the Block Island Strait, is surrounded on three quarters of its perimeter by water, wetlands and woods. The client commissioned a home that would have minimal impact on the environment, enjoy unbeatable panoramic views and offer all the comfort proper to a second home. The two volumes that make up the house, arranged in an L-shape, fulfill different functions: one contains the communal areas and the other the private ones. The dominant material, both indoors and outdoors, is wood, and its warmth provides a contrast with the coldness of the beams and pillars in the daytime areas. The scarcity and asymmetry of the openings on the façade with the entrance are compensated by the transparency of the perimeter while also offering its occupants extraordinary views.

Situé au sommet d'une colline orientée vers le détroit de Block Island, ce terrain isolé est entouré d'eau, de zones humides et de forêts sur trois côtés. Le client voulait une construction forte ayant un impact minimum sur le milieu environnant, tirant parti au maximum du paysage et dotée de toutes les commodités d'une résidence secondaire. Les deux volumes composant l'habitation, disposés en forme de L, accomplissent des fonctions différentes : l'un abrite les zones communes et l'autre les parties privées. Le bois est le matériau essentiellement utilisé à l'intérieur comme à l'extérieur. Sa chaleur se conjugue à merveille à la froideur des poutres et des colonnes des zones de jour. La rareté et l'asymétrie des ouvertures sur la façade d'accès à l'habitation sont compensées par le pourtour diaphane, tout en offrant à ses occupants un panorama et une ambiance extraordinaires.

Dieses Haus steht auf einer Anhöhe, die zu der Meerenge vor Block Island zeigt. Das einsame Grundstück ist auf fast allen Seiten von Wasser, Feuchtgebieten und Wäldern umgeben. Der Kunde wünschte sich ein Haus, das die Landschaft so wenig wie möglich unterbricht, sie ausnutzt und dennoch über allen notwendigen Komfort für einen Zweitwohnsitz verfügt. Das Gebäude besteht aus zwei in L-Form angeordneten Abschnitten, die unterschiedliche Funktionen erfüllen. In einem Flügel liegen die gemeinschaftlich bewohnten Bereiche und im anderen die privaten Räume. Sowohl innen als auch außen wurde vor allem Holz verwendet, dessen Wärme mit der Kälte der Träger und Stützen in den tagsüber genutzten Räumen kombiniert wird. Die fehlenden Öffnungen und die Asymmetrie der Fassade im Eingangsbereich werden durch die Transparenz der übrigen Fassaden ausgeglichen. Diese Transparenz lässt für die Bewohner einen wundervollen Blick und eine außergewöhnliche Stimmung entstehen.

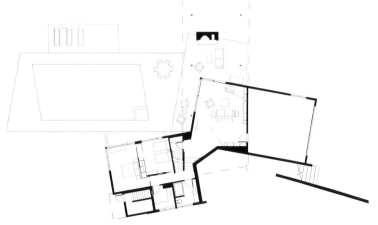

› Ground floor Rez-de-chaussée Erdgeschoss

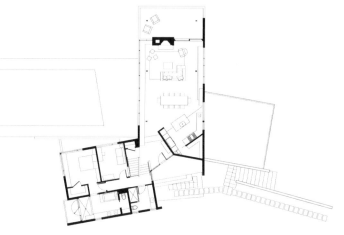

› First floor Premier étage Erstes Obergeschoss

Glass was the material most used on the façades, in order to integrate the natural landscape into the interiors of the house.

Afin que le paysage naturel qui l'entoure fasse partie des intérieurs de la maison, le verre est le matériau de prédilection des façades.

Damit die umgebende Landschaft zu einem Teil des Hauses wird, verwendete man an den Fassaden sehr viel Glas.

House in Casey Key

Maison à Casey Key

Haus in Casey Key

This vacation home is located in a rich environmental setting surronded by oak trees, palm trees and mangroves. With the Gulf of Mexico to the west and the Bay of Sarasota to the east, the house enjoys splendid views in every direction. The extreme climatic conditions greatly influenced the project's design. The house is elevated 16 feet above ground level in order to protect it from potential floods whithout interfering with the terrain. The house is reached by way of an exterior stainless steel staircase. The stairway is the project's center that unites and separates the different activities. The formal architectural repertoire and details, in a language with minimal lines, facilitate the integration of the building with its surroundings.

Cette maison de vacances est située sur un terrain riche en atmosphère, rempli de hêtres, palmiers et palétuviers. De plus, le golfe du Mexique à l'ouest et la baie de Sarasota à l'est génèrent des conditions climatiques extrêmes qui le touchent directement. En fonction de ces facteurs géoclimatiques, les architectes ont décidé d'élever le volume jusqu'à une hauteur de cinq mètres au-dessus du niveau du terrain afin de le protéger d'éventuelles inondations, une solution qui permet en outre de minimiser l'impact sur le terrain. L'accès à l'habitation s'effectue par un escalier extérieur d'acier inoxydable, cœur du projet, puisqu'il distribue l'espace. La conception formelle de l'architecture et des détails, dans un langage de lignes minimalistes, favorise l'intégration de l'édifice sur le terrain.

Dieses Ferienhaus befindet sich auf einem besonders schönen Grundstück voller Eichen, Palmen und Mangrovenbäumen. Außerdem liegt im Westen der Golf von Mexiko und im Osten die Bucht Sarasota, was zu extremen klimatischen Bedingungen führt, die den Standort direkt beeinflussen. Aufgrund dieser geoklimatischen Faktoren entschieden die Architekten, das Gebäude fünf Meter über dem Boden zu errichten, um es vor möglichen Überschwemmungen zu schützen. So wurde auch das Gelände nicht verändert. Der Zugang zum Haus erfolgt über eine Außentreppe aus Edelstahl, die gleichzeitig das Zentrum des Hauses darstellt, weil sie die verschiedenen Bereiche voneinander trennt. Die formelle Sprache der Architektur und die minimalistischen Linien sorgen für eine vollständige Integration des Gebäudes in die Umgebung.

The architects decided to raise the block to a height of 16 ft above ground level in order to make a minimal impact on the setting.

Les architectes ont décidé d'élever le volume de cinq mètres au-dessus du niveau du terrain pour réduire l'impact sur l'environnement.

Die Architekten planten das Gebäude mit einer Höhe von fünf Metern über dem Boden, damit es sich so unauffällig wie möglich in die Umgebung einfügt.

› Ground floor Rez-de-chaussée Erdgeschoss

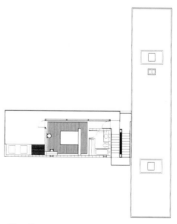

› First floor Premier étage Erstes Obergeschoss

Marshall House
Maison Marshall
Marshall Haus

This house, set in a solitary bay on the south coast of Australia, consists of a narrow concrete parallelepiped that in fact forms one side of a large, square patio covered with a lawn and bordered on its other three sides by imposing, 3-ft-high concrete walls. The walls barely seem to hold back the sand that accumulates around them and make the house totally invisible. On the east side, a path between the dunes leads to an opening that provides access to the property. Only the two rooms at each end—the sitting room and the main bedroom—open on to the northern and southern façades. The remaining bedrooms and bathrooms enjoy views of the beach via windows whose dimensions and placement are determined by specific features of the surrounding landscape.

Cette demeure, située sur une baie solitaire de la côte australienne sud, forme un étroit parallélépipède de béton qui, en réalité se présente comme un large patio carré couvert de gazon et flanqué de deux imposants murs de béton de trois mètres de haut sur ses trois autres côtés. Les murs semblent difficilement contenir le sable accumulé tout autour du périmètre, masquant parfaitement la maison. Sur le flanc est, un chemin pratiqué entre les dunes conduit à une ouverture accédant à l'intérieur. Seules les pièces situées aux extrémités – le séjour et la chambre à coucher des propriétaires – s'ouvrent sur les façades nord et sud de l'habitation. Le reste des chambres à coucher et les salles de bain jouissent de vues sur la plage grâce à des baies vitrées dont l'emplacement et les dimensions découlent des éléments concrets du paysage qu'elles encadrent.

Dieses Haus in einer einsamen Bucht an der Südküste Australiens besteht aus einem schmalen Parallelepiped aus Beton, das auch eine der Seiten des großen Innenhofes bildet. Der Boden dieses Hofes ist mit Rasen bedeckt und die anderen drei Seiten werden von gewaltigen, drei Meter hohen Mauern geschlossen. Diese Mauern scheinen den Sand, der sich um das Haus herum angehäuft hat, kaum halten zu können und lassen das Haus fast verschwinden. Auf der Ostseite führt ein Weg durch die Dünen bis zu der Öffnung, durch die man Haus und Hof erreicht. Nur die beiden Zimmer an den Enden des Gebäudes, das Wohnzimmer und das große Schlafzimmer, öffnen sich zur Nord- und Südfassade. Von den übrigen Schlafzimmern und Bädern aus schaut man durch Fenster auf den Strand, deren Anordnung und Größe von konkreten Elementen der umgebenden Landschaft bestimmt sind.

S House
Maison S
Haus S

The prevailing idea behind this architectural complex is the dialogue between full and void. Of pure geometry and contrasting materials, the house is composed of various volumes that are ordered symmetrically along an axis that materializes in a unique windowed gallery that crosses the entire building. The rhythm that produces the sequences between full and void, transparent and opaque, culminates in the house's only bedroom: an opaque block that projects itself as an oblique form, like a funnel, over the landscape. A glazed volume hangs over this block on its widest face and opens it towards the views, connecting it to the exterior. Preceding the bedroom are two translucent, symmetrical volumes, each with a bathroom and dressing room, seperated by a large glass gallery. When the sliding doors of the gallery are open, the space is transformed into a large open patio between the bedroom and the rest of the residence.

Le design de ce complexe architectural est régi par l'interaction entre les concepts de plein et de vide. Fort d'une géométrie pure et d'une palette de matériaux contrastés, cet ensemble se compose de divers volumes disposés en enfilade sur un axe matérialisé par une galerie de verre. Le rythme produit par l'alternance entre la transparence et l'opacité atteint son point culminant dans l'unique chambre à coucher de la maison : un bloc opaque qui se projette comme une forme oblique, à l'instar d'un entonnoir, sur le paysage. Un autre volume est posé sur ce bloc, avec sa façade la plus large tout en verre, lui octroyant ainsi un magnifique décor naturel et le reliant à l'extérieur. A la suite, deux volumes translucides et symétriques, chacun avec salle de bains et dressing respectifs, séparés par la galerie de verre, font office de patio entre la chambre à coucher et le reste de l'habitation dès l'ouverture des portes coulissantes.

Die Idee, die bei diesem architektonischen Komplex ausschlaggebend war, ist die Interaktion zwischen den Konzepten Leere und Fülle. Dieses Gebäude mit seiner reinen Geometrie und der dazu kontrastierenden Materialpalette besteht aus verschiedenen Blöcken, die über einer Achse angeordnet sind. Der Rhythmus, der durch sich abwechselnde Durchsichtigkeit und Undurchsichtigkeit entsteht, findet seinen Höhepunkt im Schlafzimmer des Hauses; ein Block, der sich selbst als eine schräge Form projiziert und einen Trichter über der Landschaft bildet. Über diesem Block befindet sich ein anderes Element, dessen breiteste Fassade verglast ist, so dass die Natur selbst und die Verbindung nach außen als Dekoration dient. Daran schließen sich zwei lichtdurchlässige symmetrische Blöcke an, die durch die verglaste Galerie getrennt werden. Wenn die Schiebetüren geöffnet werden, haben sie die Funktion eines Innenhofes zwischen dem Schlafzimmer und den übrigen Räumen.

The interior of this house was designed to be the opposite of the exterior, and this approach accentuates the different personalities of each area.

L'intérieur de cette résidence a été conçu comme étant le pôle opposé à l'extérieur qui l'accueille, une solution qui exalte les différences et les caractéristiques de chaque plan.

Das Innere dieses Hauses wurde als Gegenpol zu seinem äußeren Erscheinungsbild gestaltet. Diese Lösung unterstreicht die Unterschiede und Charakteristika jeder Ebene.

The geometry that governs the entire project is very simple: right angles and cubes are combined in a strict order that banishes any curves or asymmetry.

La géométrie qui domine l'ensemble du projet est très simple : angles droits et corps cubiques se mêlent à l'ordre strict sans admettre ni courbes ni asymétries.

Das Haus wird von einer sehr einfachen Geometrie geprägt: gerade Winkel und würfelförmige Körper - streng geordnet und ohne Kurven und Asymmetrien.

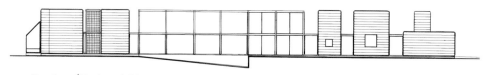

› Elevation Élévation Aufriss

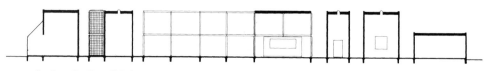

› Section Section Schnitt

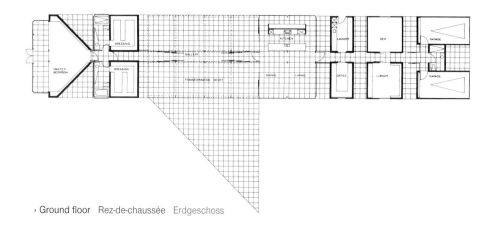

› Ground floor Rez-de-chaussée Erdgeschoss

Coromandel House
Maison Coromandel
Coromandel Haus

This lot stretching along a north-south axis is made up of two areas characterized by very different landscapes and views. The southern section is occupied by a pine forest, while the northern part enjoys more extensive views across Mercury Bay to the Great Barrier and Mercury Island in New Zealand. The lot is relatively flat, as well as being long and narrow, and two buildings were constructed along its length. The first, set in the middle of the forest, is a simple square that contains a guest bedroom, a pantry, and a play area. The main building is set closer to the northern part of the lot, to take advantage of the view of the sea, and it contains the house's daytime and night-time areas. Large sliding glass panels that can be retracted to a single point make it possible to fully integrate the living room, dining room and kitchen into the landscape.

Ce terrain, qui s'étend sur un axe nord-sud, présente deux zones donnant sur un paysage et des vues panoramiques très différentes. La partie sud accueille un bois de pins et la partie nord du terrain bénéficie de splendides panoramas allant de la baie Mercury jusque vers les îles de la Grande Barrière et Mercury, en Nouvelle Zélande. Le terrain, relativement plat, est à la fois étroit et allongé. Il accueille deux volumes qui s'étirent en longueur. Le premier, très simple et de forme carrée, situé au milieu du bois, héberge une chambre d'amis, une remise et une zone de jeux. Le volume principal, plus proche de la partie nord, bénéficie ainsi de vues panoramiques. Il abrite les zones de jour et de nuit. De grands panneaux vitrés et coulissants, ancrés en un seul endroit, permettent d'intégrer entièrement au paysage, la zone du séjour, la salle à manger et la cuisine.

Dieses Grundstück erstreckt sich über eine Nord-Süd-Achse und besteht aus zwei Bereichen, in denen sich die umgebende Landschaft und die Aussicht sehr unterscheiden. Im Süden steht ein Pinienwald und auf der Nordseite überblickt man die Mercury Bay bis zum Great Barrier Riff und die Mercury Insol in Neuseeland. Das Grundstück ist relativ eben, schmal und lang. Die Architekten errichteten zwei Gebäudeteile, die das Grundstück der Länge nach einnehmen. Eines dieser beiden Gebäude ist sehr einfach: es ist quadratisch und liegt mitten im Wald. Dieser Bau enthält das Gästezimmer, eine Speisekammer und ein Spielzimmer. Das Hauptgebäude liegt nach Norden und beherbergt die wichtigsten Wohnräume für den Tag und die Nacht. Von hier aus hat man einen wundervollen Blick über das Meer. Das Wohnzimmer, das Speisezimmer und die Küche können mithilfe großer, gläserner Schiebetüren, die an einem einzigen Punkt eingeholt werden können, miteinander verbunden werden.

› Front elevation Élévation frontale Vorderansicht

› Rear elevation Élévation arrière Hinteransicht

Residence on the Coast

Résidence sur la côte

Residenz an der Küste

Geometric interplay characterizes the distinctive forms of this house. The entrance to the house leads to a square volume containing the sitting room, marked off by sliding glass panels that enable the space to be totally exposed to the open air, albeit protected by a colossal projecting cornice. This area, which benefits from stunning views, is connected to a rectangular volume running parallel to the coastline that contains the night-time spaces. Once again, glass is the main construction material here, and this approach ensures that the entire building receives abundant sunlight. Inside, wood is the dominant element on the floors, while white sets the tone on the walls and ceilings. This luxurious house is rounded off by the harmonious, minimalist decoration.

Le jeu géométrique caractérise la volumétrie particulière de cette résidence. L'accès à l'habitation mène à un volume carré qui héberge le salon, délimité par des panneaux vitrés coulissants, qui peut être ainsi entièrement à ciel ouvert tout en étant protégé par une corniche en encorbellement. Cet endroit offre un point de vue, à couper le souffle. Un autre volume rectangulaire relié au premier qui héberge la zone de nuit s'étend en parallèle à la ligne côtière. Le verre est également le matériau de construction essentiel, moyen qui octroie à l'ensemble une grande quantité de lumière naturelle. A l'intérieur, le bois prédomine sur les sols et le blanc sur les murs et les plafonds. Une décoration minimaliste et harmonieuse exalte cette résidence parée de tous les luxes.

Das Spiel mit der Geometrie charakterisiert die eigentümlichen Formen dieses Hauses. Der Zugang zu dem Gebäude führt zu einem quadratischen Block, in dem das Wohnzimmer liegt und der von verglasten Schiebepaneelen begrenzt ist. Das Wohnzimmer kann mit diesen Paneelen vollkommen geöffnet werden und ist gleichzeitig von einem riesigen Gesims auf einem Vorsprung geschützt. Von hier aus hat man einen überwältigenden Ausblick. In einer anderen rechteckigen Form, die mit der ersten verbunden ist, befinden sicht die Schlafbereiche. Sie erstreckt sich parallel an der Küste entlang. Glas ist der dominierende Baustoff, weshalb auch sehr viel Tageslicht in das Haus fällt. Im Inneren dominieren das Holz der Böden und das Weiß der Wände und der Decken. Eine minimalistische und harmonische Dekoration macht dieses Haus, das mit allem Luxus ausgestattet ist, vollkommen.

Glass is the predominant building material, and it leads to an abundant supply of natural light.

Le verre est le matériau de construction prépondérant, solution qui offre à l'ensemble une immense quantité de lumière naturelle.

Glas ist der dominierende Baustoff, weshalb auch sehr viel Tageslicht in das Haus fällt.

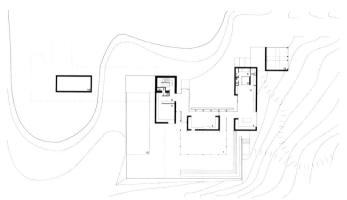

› Ground floor   Rez-de-chaussée   Erdgeschoss

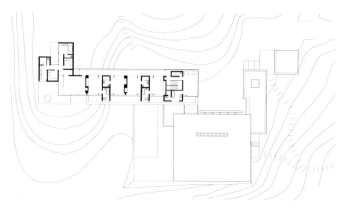

› First floor   Premier étage   Erstes Obergeschoss

House in Atami

Maison à Atami

Haus in Atami

The main purpose of the Water Glass House, situated on the Atami coast on the edge of a cliff, facing the Pacific Ocean, is for guest accommodationa. It has three floors, and occupies half of the area of a 120 square-foot plot. Although in the past years, the use of concrete as a construction element is frequent in Japanese architecture, for Kuma it is too heavy and he has set up the principle of transparency against the use of this material. The floor of the lowest level is covered by a layer of water 35" deep. Three bodies of glass, two square and one oval, have been placed over it and are reflected in the water. They are covered by a metal slat roof. Wherever possible, Kuma has used glass as the construction material. The walls have lost density and have been converted into filters. The intention was that people should have the sensation of floating on water.

Cette construction, située au bord d'une falaise face à l'océan Pacifique, a la fonction essentielle de loger des invités. Dotée de trois étages, elle occupe la moitié de la superficie d'un terrain de 1.281 m². Si l'emploi du béton dans l'architecture japonaise est de plus en plus fréquent, Kuma juge ce matériau trop lourd et utilise ce projet pour instaurer un principe de transparence. Le sol du niveau inférieur est recouvert d'une couche d'eau de 15 cm de profondeur. Trois volumes de verre – deux carrés et un ovale – semblent flotter sur cette surface liquide. D'une manière générale, le principe de cette construction montre que, chaque fois que cela est possible, Kuma utilise le verre comme matériau de construction. Il s'ensuit que les murs, moins épais, se transforment en filtres. L'objectif de l'architecte est de donner aux hôtes la sensation de flotter sur l'eau.

Die wichtigste Funktion dieses Hauses am Rande einer Steilküste am Pazifischen Ozean ist, den Gästen Unterkunft zu gewähren. Das Haus hat drei Stockwerke und nimmt die Hälfte eines 1281 m² großen Grundstücks ein. Obwohl in den letzten Jahren immer mehr Beton in der japanischen Architektur verwendet wurde, vertritt Kuma die Ansicht, dass es sich um ein zu schweres Material handelt. Deshalb setzte er bei diesem Haus das Prinzip der Transparenz um. Auf der unteren Ebene bedeckte er den Boden mit einem 15 cm tiefen Wasserstreifen. Drei Formen aus Glas, zwei davon quadratisch und eine eiförmig, scheinen sich auf dieser flüssigen Oberfläche widerzuspiegeln. Kuma verwendete an diesem Gebäude, wenn es möglich war, Glas, so dass die Wände ihre Dichte verloren haben und zu Filtern wurden. Das Ziel des Architekten war, den Gästen das Gefühl zu geben, auf dem Wasser zu treiben.

This structure seeks to make its occupant feel as though he is floating on water.

Le but de cette structure est que l'hôte se sente flotter sur l'eau.

Es wurde eine Struktur geschaffen, in der sich der Gast fühlt, als ob er auf dem Wasser treiben würde.

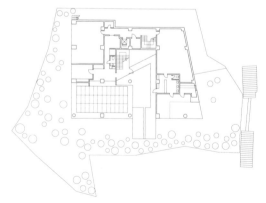

› Location plan Plan de situation Umgebungsplan

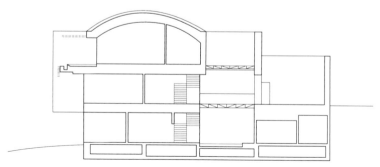

› Section Section Schnitt

› Ground floor Rez-de-chaussée Erdgeschoss

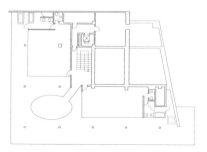

› First floor Premier étage Erstes Obergeschoss

The house is directly connected to the parking lot via a steel and concrete bridge.

On accède à la maison directement par le parking à travers un pont d'acier et de béton.

Man betritt das Haus über eine Brücke aus Stahl und Beton direkt vom Parkplatz aus.

Photo Credits   Crédits photographiques   Fotonachweis